THE COMPLETE BOOK
OF BIBLE STORIES
FOR JEWISH CHILDREN

from CREATION to JOSHUA
PART ONE

W9-BMA-952

from JOSHUA to JUDAH MACCABEE
PART TWO

by
DAVID DANIEL

illustrated by
Ben Einhorn

KTAV PUBLISHING HOUSE INC.

Design and art supervision by EZEKIEL SCHLOSS

SBN 87068-381-0
© COPYRIGHT 1971
KTAV PUBLISHING HOUSE, INC.

Manufactured in the United States of America
Library of Congress Catalog Card Number: 75-155841

THE JEWISH BEGINNING

from CREATION to JOSHUA

PART ONE

by
DAVID DANIEL

illustrated by
Ben Einhorn

KTAV PUBLISHING HOUSE INC.

TABLE OF CONTENTS

from CREATION to JOSHUA

THE CREATION

How did the world begin? Who made it? Why, God made the world, of course! And why did God make the world? Because God is the Great Creator, from whom everything good and wonderful comes. It gave Him great joy to create something as beautiful as the world. God made our beautiful world and then he set it spinning in space.

In the beginning, there was no light at all in the world, so God said, "Let there be light," and there was light. And God called the light, "Day" and the dark, "Night." And that was the very first day in the world.

God loved the world so much, and He was so proud of it, that He gave it every wondrous thing He thought of. On the second day, God divided the world into two parts. The upper half was the sky and the air, which is spread over the earth like a tent. He made the clouds too, which sometimes, filled with water, come down upon the earth as rain. The lower half of the world was below the sky and was a mass of dark water.

On the third day, God separated the waters from the dry land and He called the dry land "Earth." The waters became mighty oceans and rivers and brooks and waterfalls. Now the ground was ready for trees, flowers and grass, so God made them next. How changed the earth looked now! The most wonderful painter who ever lived could never paint a color as beautiful as the colors God gave the world. There were red, red roses, yellow daffodils, purple asters, orange sunflowers, and blue forget-me-nots. God made the tall trees and He gave the world all kinds of food for the people who were going to live there. It is very easy to see that He loved His world very much, because He made all the food so delicious.

God made many different kinds of foods. Now, He did not have to do this, but He made wonderful juicy grapes, sweet purple plums, golden corn, red apples, and crisp green lettuce and . . . why, there are so many different kinds of foods to eat that it would take a whole book just

to name them all. Just stop and think how many different and wonderful tastes there are in this world.

On the fourth day, God made His world even more beautiful. He created the sun and the moon and the twinkling stars. The sun to give light and warmth to the earth by day, and the moon to give a soft, restful light at night. The stars seemed to sparkle, and when God looked at the stars it seemed to Him they were laughing with joy, and God was pleased, because He looked all around Him and He saw that His world was good!

On the fifth day, God put the first living creatures upon the earth. He filled the oceans, the rivers, and the brooks with all kinds of wonderful fish and animals of all sizes and shapes, from the huge whale to the tiny minnow. And He filled the air with beautiful birds of all kinds and colors; red birds and blue birds, and wonderful tropical birds with feathers of the brightest green, yellow, red, and gold; friendly robins and tiny wrens and sparrows and hummingbirds. The world became filled with color and music as the beautiful fish swam through the clear waters and the birds sang their lovely songs.

On the sixth day God made the animals of the earth; the gentle cows, woolly sheep, huge elephants, and furry kittens. All the animals loved each other: the graceful and gentle deer were not afraid of the fierce wolves and tigers. Everyone lived in peace and harmony. And once more God looked about Him and saw that the world was good.

I want you to notice how wisely God created everything. He did not make the fish before He made the seas for them to swim in. He did not make the birds before He made the air and the trees. Trees and flowers cannot live without air, so God made the air before He made them. God did not make the animals before He made the grass for them to eat; but the whole world was created in its right order.

ADAM AND EVE

But there were no people in the world—no cities nor houses, and no children playing under the trees. The world was all ready for men and women to enjoy it: and so God said, "I will make man to be different from all other animals. He shall stand upright on his feet, and he shall have a soul, and shall be like God; and he shall be the master of the earth and all that is upon it."

So God made man from the dust of the ground, and breathed into him the breath of life; and man became alive and stood up on the earth.

And so that the man whom God had made might have a home, God planted a beautiful garden on the earth at a place where four rivers met in Eden. In this garden He planted trees and caused grass to grow and made flowers to bloom. God gave this "Garden of Eden" to the man whom he had made, and told him to care for it, and to gather the fruits upon the trees and the plants, eat them, and live upon them. And God gave the first man the name, Adam: and God brought to Adam all the animals that he had made and let Adam give to each one its name.

But Adam was all alone in this beautiful garden. And God said, "It is not good for man to be alone. I will make someone to be with Adam and to help him." So when Adam was asleep, God took a rib from Adam's side, and from it God made a woman; and he brought her to Adam, and Adam called her Eve. And Adam and Eve loved one another; and they were happy in the beautiful garden which God had given them for a home.

This was the end of the sixth day and God was very pleased with His world and His creatures. He decided that on the seventh day, He would rest. So God blessed the Seventh Day and called it the Sabbath. Adam and Eve also rested on the Sabbath and they walked quietly among God's creations, thinking how good it felt just to be alive in God's wonderful new world.

And this is a good thing for everyone to think on the Sabbath Day, and every day! For if you just stop and look around you, you will see hundreds of different things that remind you that God is always thinking of you and caring for you. God sends the sunshine and rain to make our food grow; He gives us the daytime for work and happy play, and the night for restful sleep. He has given us the power of speech, so that we can talk and laugh and be happy with all our friends. God has, indeed, been good to us.

THE SERPENT IN THE GARDEN

In the middle of the Garden of Eden God planted two trees; one was the Tree of Life and the other was the Tree of the Knowledge of Good and Evil. God said to Adam and Eve: "You may eat the fruit of all the trees in the garden except the fruits from the Tree of Good and Evil. If you eat of the fruit upon that tree, you shall die."

Eve could not help being curious. She would walk around the tree and stare at it, wondering to herself exactly what would happen if she were to eat one of the big rosy apples hanging from the branches. One morning, while Adam was swimming in one of the beautiful brooks in the Garden, Eve stole quietly away to the place where the Tree of the Knowledge of Good and Evil grew. How beautiful were the apples on this tree! They sparkled brightly in the sunlight. Eve could smell

their perfume and her mouth began to water as she imagined how crisp and sweet they would taste. But then she remembered what God had said and she felt ashamed. She started to turn away, when suddenly she heard a hissing noise. She glanced down at the trunk of the tree. There, curled around its foot, was a snake, with green scales that glistened in the sunlight, and sharp black eyes. Then the serpent spoke.

"I saw you looking at the apples on this tree," it said, in a hissing voice. "Why do you not eat one?".

Eve swallowed hard and spoke in a weak and trembling voice.

"God has commanded us not to eat of the fruit of this tree," she answered.

The snake gave a long, hissing laugh.

"Of course God has told you not to eat of this fruit, you foolish woman," said the snake. "But do you know why?"

"It is not for us to question God's commands, but to obey them. For God sends only good to His creatures."

The serpent laughed scornfully. He was very cunning and sly.

"Fools!" he hissed. "Do you not know that if you ate this fruit you would be as wise as God, and have as much knowledge as He has? That is why God does not want you to eat this fruit. He is afraid you will be as powerful as He is! Think how it would feel to be as knowing and as powerful as God Himself!"

The snake kept looking at Eve with his black eyes and Eve kept staring back. Then she looked at the apples on the tree. They were red and beautiful as they hung on the branches and smelled sweeter than honey. Eve reached out, picked one of the apples and took a great bite, and offered the apple to Adam, too. Never had she tasted such fruit.

The apple looked cool and juicy and it smelled delicious. Adam took the apple, too, and ate it all.

Suddenly the Garden was filled with the sound of God's voice:

"Adam, where art thou?"

Adam and Eve fell to the ground and trembled. They knew this was God's voice, and they knew they had done wrong. For the first time, their hearts were greatly troubled.

The Lord God called to Adam, saying, "Where are you?"

"I heard Your voice in the garden," said Adam, "and I was afraid because I was naked, and I hid myself."

"Who told you that you were naked?" asked the Lord God. "Have you eaten of the tree whose fruit I commanded you not to eat?"

Adam said, "The woman whom you gave me to be with me, she gave me the fruit, and I ate."

Then the Lord God said to the woman, "What is this you have done?"

And the woman said, "The serpent tempted me, and I ate."

Then the Lord God said to the serpent, "Because you have done this, you are cursed above all cattle and above every beast of the field. You shall crawl on your belly and eat dust all the days of your life. I shall make the woman and her children enemies of you and of your children through the years."

Then God looked at Adam and Eve with great sadness, for He had tried so hard to give them all good things, and they had turned from Him and had forgotten Him.

"Now you have eaten the fruit of the Tree of the Knowledge of Good and Evil," God said. "From this day forward, your hearts will know sorrow as well as joy. If you want food, you must dig and plant and reap and work as long as you live. You came from the ground, for you were made of dust, and back again into the dust shall your body go when you die."

And because Adam and Eve had disobeyed the word of the Lord, they were driven out of the beautiful Garden of Eden, which God had made to be their home. They were sent out into the world; and to keep them from going back into the garden, God placed his angels before its gate, with swords which flashed like fire to guard the Tree of Life so that no man could eat its fruit.

CAIN AND ABEL

Even though Adam and Eve had to leave the beautiful Garden of Eden, they soon had something else to be very happy about. They had two beautiful baby sons, Cain and Abel.

Adam and Eve watched their sons grow up to be fine, strong men. Adam taught Cain how to plough the ground and plant seeds and raise fruits and vegetables. He taught Abel how to care for sheep.

But though Cain and Abel were both strong and healthy, there was one great difference between them. Cain did not like his work. It made him angry when he had to dig hard in the soil. He hated carrying the heavy sacks of grain, and the baskets of fruits and vegetables at harvest time. You see, instead of blessing the soil as he ploughed, and thanking God for the wonderful food that would grow from the tiny seeds, Cain grumbled and complained all the time he worked.

But Abel loved his work. He loved every sheep in his flock, and when the little lambs were born, Abel cared for them tenderly. He never forgot to thank God for blessing him with so many fine, fat sheep.

It was the custom in that long-ago time to offer sacrifices to God to thank Him for His goodness. Abel decided one day to give God his finest lamb. He picked the little fellow up in his arms and patted its curly head.

"I shall give you to God, little lamb," he said, "for He has been good to me and I am very grateful!"

Cain also offered a sacrifice to God, but he offered the worst of his fruits and vegetables for the sacrifice. The apples were withered and many of them were full of worms. The grapes were small and sour. The vegetables were pale and scrawny.

When Cain arrived at the place where the sacrifices were made, he found Abel already there with his fine fat lamb.

"What are you doing here?" asked Cain.

"I think it is only fair that I give God back a part of what He has given me," answered his brother.

Then Abel noticed that Cain was holding something behind his back.

"What is that you are carrying?" he asked.

Cain's face became very red as he brought forth the basket of withered fruits and vegetables for Abel to see. Abel tried to admire the poor offering, because he did not want to hurt Cain's feelings.

"Oh, you have brought a sacrifice, too!" he said. "That's good! Now God will bless your land and give you fine big plums and apples, and a rich harvest of grain!"

But suddenly, as Cain looked at Abel's fat little lamb, and then at his own poor offering, he was so ashamed that he flung his basket to the ground. The fruits and vegetables rolled in every direction!

"I do not need to be blessed!" shouted Cain. "My offering is just as good as yours! You think you are so fine with your fat lamb!"

Cain became so angry that he picked up a stone and threw it with all his might at his brother, hitting him with the stone. Abel gave him one startled glance, then fell to the ground.

Cain was frightened at what he had done. He was no longer angry, only sorry. He ran to Abel and knelt on the ground beside him, sobbing:

"What have I done! I have killed my own brother!"

Then he quickly buried Abel's body. But when he had finished, he heard a mighty voice crying:

"Where is Abel, your brother?"

Cain trembled, for he knew this was the voice of God.

"I do not know," Cain answered. "Am I my brother's keeper?"

God's voice became very stern, and he cried:

"Your brother's blood cries to me from the ground! What have you done?"

Cain buried his face in his hands, and God spoke again:

"You have spilled your brother's blood into the earth. No more will the earth give you fruits and vegetables and grain! You must wander as a vagabond from place to place from this day on!"

And Cain said to the Lord, "My punishment is greater than I can bear. You have driven me out from among men. If any man finds me, he will kill me, because I shall be alone, and no one will be my friend."

But God put a mark upon Cain's forehead so that no harm would come to him, and then told him he must begin his weary wandering from place to place, never resting.

After many years, Cain prayed to God and asked to be forgiven. God knew that Cain was truly sorry for his sin, so He forgave him, and Cain lived in the Land of Nod until he was a very old man, and married and had children.

THE FLOOD

Have you ever seen a rainbow, stretching like a beautiful bridge across the sky? Have you ever wondered about it? This is the story of why God put the very first rainbow in the sky.

After Adam and Eve had been banished by God from the Garden of Eden, they had many children. These children also had children, and God's new world was soon filled with many people. But instead of being thankful for the wonderful fruits and grain, and the beautiful flowers, and the world God had created for them, these people became more and more selfish and wicked. They forgot all about God.

God's heart was filled with sorrow when He saw how ugly people were making His beautiful world. He became very angry. God was pleased, however, that there was at least one man who was good and kind. That man was Noah. Even though Noah lived in the midst of wicked people, he did not allow their sinfulness to turn him from his good ways.

One day, while Noah was walking in his fields, he heard a voice. He began to tremble, for the voice came out of the sky like a great roll of thunder, and it said:

"I have decided to put an end to all human beings. They have filled the earth with violence. I will destroy them and the earth together. Make yourself an ark of wood. Build rooms in the ark and cover it inside and outside with pitch. Make a roof for it and, in it, a window, and put the doorway of the ark in its side; also put three decks in it. For I am sending a flood of waters on the earth, to destroy every living creature under heaven; everything on earth shall perish."

And God continued to speak to Noah:

"But I will make a covenant with you; you shall enter the ark accompanied by your sons, Shem, Ham, and Japheth, your wife, and your sons' wives. And you shall bring into the ark male and female of every living thing: seven pairs of clean creatures, fit for sacrifice and needed by men, of every kind, to keep along with you. And of the beasts that are not clean, domestic animals and

every kind of beast and bird, you shall take two pairs, the male and his mate, that they may be kept alive. Go now and gather every kind of edible food, and store it away to be food for you and for them."

Noah thanked God, and then he went to tell his sons he was going to build an ark and that they must help him. One of his sons said to his brother, "Do you suppose that our father is getting so old that he doesn't know what he is doing? Where is this ark to sail when it is built? Across the fields on the waves of grain?"

But his brother shook his head and answered,

"Our father has never commanded us to do anything wrong. He is very wise and good. Therefore, let us help him build his ark as we should."

And Noah did what God told him to do, although it must have seemed very strange to all the people around to see them build this great ark where there was no water for it to sail upon. It was a long time that Noah and his sons were at work building the ark, while the wicked people around wondered and, no doubt, laughed at Noah for building a great ship where there was no sea.

Noah pleaded with them to return to God but the foolish people just laughed. At last the ark was finished, and stood like a great house on the land. There was a door

on one side, and a window on the roof, to let in the light. Then God said to Noah, "Come into the ark, you and your wife, and your three sons, and their wives with them; for the flood of waters will come very soon. And take with you the animals of all kinds, and birds and things that creep, so that all kinds of animals may be kept alive upon the earth."

So Noah and his wife, and his three sons, Shem, Ham, and Japheth, with their wives, went into the ark. Everyone helped to carry in the food that was to be stored for the time when the flood would come. Even the children carried in loaves of bread and apples and dried fruit. Then Noah led the animals into the ark. In his great thoughtfulness and wisdom he had even built a special room in the ark with a ceiling much higher than the others. Can you guess why? For the two giraffes, of course!

Then it began to rain. For forty days and forty nights,

the water poured from the heavens. Houses were torn from their foundations and floated away on the water, and great trees were uprooted. People suddenly remembered God, and called to Him to save them, but it was too late. The rain fell in great torrents, until the water covered all the earth, and every living creature had perished. The waters covered the tallest trees and the highest mountains. But Noah and his family and all the animals were safe and snug in the ark, for it sailed upon the surface of the waters.

At first, Noah and his wife and family were afraid the ark would sink, and were very frightened when the ark pitched and rocked upon the waves, but they soon became calm, because they knew God was watching over them. Through the window in the ark, Noah could see empty houses floating past, and he felt very sad and sorry that the people in the world had been so wicked and brought about this terrible flood.

THE RAINBOW IN THE SKY

Finally, after forty days had passed, the rains stopped and Noah's ark came to rest upon one of the mountains of Ararat. Noah, seeing that the rains had stopped, opened the window of the ark and sent forth a raven into the world. But the bird flew back and forth, back and forth, and finally grew weary because it could find no resting place, and came back to the ark.

Noah knew that the waters had not yet dried up, and he waited several days and then sent forth a dove. But the dove found no treetop in which to rest and she, too, came back, and Noah put out his hand and took her back into the ark. He knew that the waters still covered the earth.

He waited seven more days, and sent the dove forth again. This time, she flew back to the ark with a green olive leaf, freshly plucked, in her mouth. Noah knew then that the trees were now above the waters. He waited still another seven days and sent the dove forth a third time.

This time she did not return, and Noah knew she had found a nesting place somewhere out in the world. Noah removed the covering of the ark, and saw that the ground had dried.

Then God spoke to Noah once more, and told him to leave the ark with his family and all the animals, and begin life anew.

Noah's heart was filled with joy, and he was so thankful that he built an altar and made a sacrifice to God. It was at that moment that a wonderful thing happened. While Noah was sacrificing at the altar, he heard God's voice, which said to Noah and his sons:

"Behold, I set My bow in the cloud. This is My promise to you, and to your children, and to all the animals and beasts of the earth that are with you: never again will the waters become a flood to destroy all flesh."

And lo and behold! A great bow stretched across the sky, with so many lovely colors that Noah and his family could only stand and gaze in wonder! It was God's first rainbow, and a sign of His promise to Noah and to all living things.

THE TOWER OF BABEL

After the great flood, the family of Noah and those who came after him grew in number until, as the years went on, the earth began to be full of people once more.

From Mount Ararat, where the ark rested, many of the people moved eastward into a country between two great rivers, the Tigris and the Euphrates; and there they built houses for themselves. They undertook to build a great city, which should rule all the peoples around them. They found that the soil in that country could be made into bricks, and that the bricks could be heated and made hard, so that it was easy to build houses to live in and to erect walls around their city.

But sometimes, when things go well for a long time, people become careless and selfish. This is exactly what happened to the people who lived soon after the great flood. It had been a long time since God had sent the waters to cover the earth. People had almost forgotten about this terrible time. They heard their great-grand-fathers and great-grandmothers talking about it, but they did not pay much attention. The people thought they were very clever indeed, and that they did not need God's help.

"Let us build a great tower!" they cried. "A tower that reaches clear to Heaven!"

"Yes! Yes!" they all shouted. "Let us build a tower to Heaven, and then we shall be as mighty as God!"

And so the tower was begun. Many men helped to build it, and as the bricks began to pile up, the tower grew taller and taller. Finally it was so tall that the people on the ground looked like ants to the men working at the top of the tower.

But the people forgot that Someone was watching them build this tower. Someone who sees everything, and even cares about what the smallest bird does.

That Someone was God.

"I shall go down to see this great tower the people are building," said God to Himself.

But when God saw how proud the people were, and how they had forgotten Him and were thinking only about their own cleverness and this foolish tower, He was very angry!

"How dare these people think they can build a tower as high as Heaven!" cried God. "I must think of some way to punish them so they will stop being so vain and selfish!"

In the meantime, the tower was becoming higher and higher.

"Look! Look!" cried the people. "The tower is taller than the tallest tree! We are greater than God, for we have built something much taller than anything He has ever made!"

Then a very strange thing happened!

"I am going to climb to the top of the tower!" cried one of the men.

"What did you say?" asked another man.

"Why are you two men making those strange sounds?" cried a third man.

And a fourth man turned to his brother and said:

"What is wrong with those men? They sound like monkeys chattering!"

But his brother looked at him in a puzzled way and said:

"I cannot understand a word you are saying!"

God had sent His punishment! He had put a strange language in every man's mouth, so that nobody understood anybody else. The people became so confused, they ran about like frightened geese, making strange noises at each other. Of course they could not build the tower any higher, for how could people build anything together when they could not speak the same language and couldn't understand one another?

The great Tower of Babel was never finished, and the people were scattered over the earth, each family settling in a different place and speaking a different tongue. That is how the different nations started, each with its own language.

ABRAM AND LOT

Not far from the city of Babylon, where they had begun to build the tower of Babel, was another city called Ur, of the Chaldees. The Chaldees lived in the country where the two rivers, Euphrates and Tigris come together. Among these people, at Ur, there lived a man called Abram.

Abram was a very good and wise man and rich, as well, but he became very unhappy when he looked around him at his neighbors. They worshiped idols and cared nothing about God. Abram prayed to God for help in finding a new home where he could raise his family in God's service. Abram's prayers were answered, for God said to him:

"Abram, gather together all your family and leave this place, and go to a land far away that I will show you. And in that land I will make your family become a great people, and I will bless you and make your name great, so that all the world shall give honor to your name. If you will do as I command you, you shall be blessed, and all the families of the earth shall obtain a blessing through you."

Although Abram did not know just what the blessing was to be that God promised to give him, and although he did not know where the land was to which God was sending him, he obeyed God's word. He took all his family and with them his father Terah, who was very old, and his wife, whose name was Sarai, and another brother's son, whose name was Lot. And Abram took all that he had, his tents and his flocks of sheep and herds of cattle, and went forth on a long journey to a land of which he did not even know the name.

He journeyed far up the great river Euphrates to the mountain region, until he came to a place called Haran, in a country called Mesopotamia. The word Mesopotamia means "between the rivers"; and this country was between the two great rivers Tigris and Euphrates. At Haran they all stayed for a time. Perhaps they stopped there because Terah, Abram's father, was too old to travel farther, for they stayed at Haran until Terah died.

After the death of Terah, his father, Abram again went on his journey; and Lot, his brother's son, went with him.

From Haran, Abram and Lot turned toward the southwest and journeyed for a long time, having the mountains on their right hand and the great desert on their left. They crossed over rivers and climbed the hills,

and at last they came into the land of Canaan, which was the land of which God had spoken to Abram.

But Abram and his people did not go into the towns to live. They lived in tents, out in the open fields, where they could find grass for their sheep and cattle. Not far from a city called Shechem, Abram set up his tent under an oak tree on the plain. There the Lord came to Abram, and said:

"I will give this land to your children and to their children, and this shall be their land forever."

And Abram built an altar there and made an offering, and worshiped the Lord. Wherever Abram set up his tent, there he built his altar and prayed to God; for Abram loved God and served God and believed God's promises.

Both Abram and Lot settled down in this rich and wonderful country of Canaan. They both had plenty of fat, healthy sheep. They both grew rich, and they were very happy. Their families lived peacefully together.

All went well for a time, but one day, one of Lot's shepherds came to him and said:

"It is not fair! Your uncle's sheep are eating all the grass and drinking all the water! There is not enough room for all these sheep!"

Shortly after this, one of Abram's shepherds came to him and said:

"Your nephew's sheep eat all the grass, while yours grow thin! They will die of thirst, for there is not enough water for all the sheep!"

Abram and Lot tried to tell the shepherds there was plenty for all. But Lot's shepherds began to quarrel with Abram's shepherds and Abram was very troubled. He was a man of peace and hated quarrels. So he said to his nephew, Lot:

"Let there be no quarrel between you and me nor between your men and my men, for you and I are like brothers to each other. The whole land is before us; let us part. You shall have the first choice. If you will take the land on the right hand, then I will take the land on the left; or if you choose the land on the left, then I will take the right."

This was noble and generous of Abram, for he was the older and could have claimed the first choice.

Lot looked over the land, and he decided that he would settle on the great plain of the River Jordan. This land was unusually beautiful, and the soil was very fertile with plenty of water. The flowers and vegetables that grew there were large and perfect.

"I will tell my uncle that I will settle on that land," said Lot to himself. When he told Abram that he had decided to live on the plain of Jordan, Abram said:

"Yes, the land is beautiful, and there is no richer soil to be found anywhere! But remember, too, that the two cities of Sodom and Gomorrah are also on the plain of Jordan. The people in these cities are very wicked. They worship idols. They know nothing of God and they do not care to know of Him. Do you think you can be happy living among these wicked people?"

But Lot shrugged his shoulders and said:

"What other people do is none of my business. All I care about is the land. My sheep need plenty of grass and I need rich soil for my gardens. I have chosen this land and there I will stay!"

And so Lot took his wife and children and moved away to the new land he had chosen. Little did he dream that the day would come when he would remember what his uncle Abram had said about the wicked cities of Sodom and Gomorrah!

Abram stayed in the land of Canaan and everyone loved him, for he was a very kind and peaceful man. God loved Abram, too. After Lot had left to go to his new home, God said to Abram:

"Lift up your eyes from this place and look east and west and north and south. All the land that you can see, mountains and valleys and plains, I will give to you and to your children and their children and those who come after them. Your descendants shall have all this land, and they shall be as many as the dust of the earth; so that if one could count the dust of the earth, they could as easily count those who shall come from you. Rise up and walk through the land wherever you please, for it is all yours."

Then Abram moved his tent from Bethel, and went to live near the city of Hebron, in the south, by the oak trees, and there again he built an altar to the Lord.

SODOM AND GOMORRAH

When Lot had decided to live on the plain of the River
Jordan, Abraham had warned him about the wicked cities
of Sodom and Gomorrah. God also saw how wicked the
people were in these two cities, and God spoke to Abraham about this one day:

"I am going to destroy Sodom and Gomorrah," He
said, "because they are wicked. The people worship idols
and care nothing for Me!"

Abraham was a compassionate man, and he worried
very much about his nephew Lot, who lived near the
gates of Sodom, and he could not bear the thought that so
many people would die. Abraham appealed to God.

"If there were fifty good men in Sodom, would you
destroy it?" Abraham asked God.

"If there are fifty good men, I will spare the city,"
God answered.

Abraham continued to reduce the number of people. Then he asked:

"But what if there are only ten good men in the city. Would you destroy it then?"

"No," said God. "If there are ten good men in the city, I will not destroy it!"

But alas, the only good man to be found in either city was Abraham's nephew, Lot.

One evening, two men came to Lot's house. Lot arose to greet them, and said:

"Come into my house and have food and rest!"

In the morning they told Lot that they had been sent by God, and they said to Lot:

"Take your wife and all your children and go away from this place. For God has sent us to destroy the cities of Sodom and Gomorrah, because the people are so wicked."

Lot hurried to tell his sons-in-law the news, but they just laughed at him and told him he must be mad to say such a thing.

Lot went back to his house and said to the angels:

"My sons-in-law have mocked me and called me a fool. They will not leave the city!"

Then Lot's wife spoke and said:

"I do not want to leave my home, either. I do not want to go away from all my friends and wander about looking for a new place to live. I love my home and I want to stay!"

Poor Lot did not know what to do. But one of the angels took Lot and his wife by the hands. The other angel took the hands of Lot's two daughters, and they pulled them out of the house and took them to the gates of the city.

"Go!" cried the angels. "And whatever you do, do not look back! Flee to the hills, lest you be swept away!"

Then God sent a great rain of fire upon the cities of the plain, and every living thing perished in the flames.

As Lot and his family hurried across the plain, Lot's wife said to him:

"Please, stop for just a moment. For I must turn to look just once more at my old home!"

"No! No!" cried Lot. "God said we must not look back!"

But alas! Lot's warning came too late His wife had turned her head to look back, and Lot was horrified to see her turn into a pillar of salt right before his eyes!

And so Lot had only his two daughters left. Together the three fugitives journeyed to the mountains, where they lived in a lonely cave.

That day, as soon as the sun came up, Abraham arose and went out to the place where he said his morning prayers. When he looked across the plain toward Sodom and Gomorrah, he saw smoke coming up from the two cities like the smoke from a mighty furnace.

HAGAR AND ISHMAEL

Abram and his wife Sarai lived happily for many years in the land of Canaan. The soil was fertile, there was plenty of grass for the sheep and cattle, and Abram grew very rich. But he never forgot to thank God for sending him so many blessings.

There was just one thing that made Abram unhappy. He and his wife Sarai had no children.

Sarai would weep and say to Abram:

"When we are old, we will have no grandchildren to bring us joy and comfort. When we die, who will carry on your name? I wish God would send me a son!"

Abram would try to comfort Sarai, but he, too, wanted a son more than anything in the world.

One night God appeared to Abram and said:

"Fear not, Abram; I am your shield; your reward shall be very great."

Abram said:

"O Lord God, what will You give me, seeing I have no children?"

Then God said:

"Look now toward heaven, and count the stars, if you can. So numerous shall your descendants be."

And Abram believed in the Lord.

But the years passed, and no son came to Abram and Sarai. Sarai wept again and said:

"I do not think I will ever have a son, for I am growing old."

Now in that time long ago, the law said that a man could have more than just one wife. Sarai wanted a child in her house so badly, and she loved Abram so much and wanted so much for him to be happy too, that she said to him one day:

"Abram, take my servant Hagar for your wife. Perhaps she will have the child we want so badly."

Abram married Hagar, and a son was born to them. The little boy was called Ishmael, and Abram was very proud of his wild, handsome son. Abram tried hard to teach him about God, and kindness and goodness, but, although Ishmael was tall and strong and handsome, he was not obedient.

THE BIRTH OF ISAAC

Sarai still had no child of her own.

When Abram was encamped near Hebron the Lord came to him and said:

"I am the Almighty God; walk before me and be perfect, and I will make you a father of many nations. And your name shall be changed. You shall no more be called Abram, but Abraham, a word that means 'Father of a multitude,' because you shall be the father of many nations of people. And your wife's name shall also be changed. She shall no more be called Sarai, but Sarah; that is, 'Princess.' And you and Sarah shall have a son, and you shall call his name Isaac; and he shall have sons when he becomes a man, and his descendants, those who spring from him, shall be very many people."

So from this time he was no longer Abram, but Abraham, and his wife was called Sarah.

One hot day, as Abraham sat in the doorway of his tent, he saw three strangers standing before him. Abraham jumped quickly to his feet and bowed.

"Come into my tent," he said kindly, "you are tired and the sun is hot today!"

Then Abraham called his servants and told them to wash the strangers' feet. Then he prepared food and cool drinks for them.

After the three men had rested and eaten, they smiled at Abraham, and such a bright light shone from their faces that Abraham could not look at them. Then one of the strangers spoke:

"Where is your wife?"

Abraham answered:

"In the tent."

"God has sent His blessing to you, Abraham; your prayers have been answered. Soon Sarah shall have a son!"

Although it was hard to believe, because Abraham and Sarah were old, Abraham shouted with joy. For now he knew that these strangers were really three angels whom God had sent to him with this great news.

The three angels went away, and Abraham called Sarah and told her the glad news. When Sarah learned that, at last, after all these years, she was to have a son, the tears rolled down her face, and she laughed aloud with joy.

God kept His promise and when a beautiful little boy was born to Abraham and Sarah, they called him Isaac, which means "laughter."

But there were two people in Abraham's family who did not laugh for joy when Isaac was born. Those two were Hagar and Ishmael. Hagar was jealous, and afraid Isaac would be heir to all of Abraham's riches. Ishmael hated little Isaac, and teased him when nobody was looking.

But Sarah could see what was happening, and she told Abraham he must send Ishmael away.

"How can I send my own son from my house?" asked Abraham.

Then Abraham asked God to help him with this problem, and God said:

"Send your son Ishmael away. I shall see that no harm comes to him; I shall make him the father of another nation."

So the next morning, Abraham sent Hagar and her boy away, expecting them to go back to the land of Egypt, from which Hagar had come. He gave them some food for the journey and a bottle of water to drink by the way. The bottles in that country were not like ours, made of

glass. They were made from the skin of a goat, sewed tightly together. One of these skin bottles Abraham filled with water and gave to Hagar.

And Hagar went away from Abraham's tent, leading her little boy. But somehow she lost her way and wandered over the desert, not knowing where she was, until all the water in the bottle was used up; and her poor boy, in the hot sun and the burning sand, had nothing to drink. She thought that he would die of his terrible thirst, and she laid him down under a little bush; and then she went away, for she said to herself:

"I cannot bear to look at my poor boy suffering and dying for want of water."

And just at that moment, while Hagar was crying and her boy was moaning with thirst, she heard a voice saying to her:

"Hagar, what is your trouble? Do not be afraid. God has heard your cry and the cry of your child. God will take care of you both, and will make of your boy a great nation of people."

It was the voice of an angel from heaven; and then Hagar looked, and there close at hand was a spring of water in the desert. How glad Hagar was, as she filled the bottle with water and took it to her suffering boy under the bush!

After this, Hagar did not go down to Egypt. She found a place near this spring, where she lived and brought up her son in the wilderness, far from other people. And God was with Ishmael and cared for him.

Ishmael became the father of the Arabian people.

ABRAHAM AND ISAAC

Isaac grew strong and tall and Abraham loved him deeply. But sometimes God tests our faith and love to see how strong and true we are. The test God gave to Abraham was a very hard one. But even though it nearly broke Abraham's heart to do what God had asked of him, he obeyed. And no wonder Abraham was heartbroken! For this is what God had said to him:

"Abraham, take your son Isaac and go into the land of Moriah and when you come to the mountain about which I shall tell you, make of your son Isaac a burnt-offering to Me!"

Abraham could scarcely believe his ears. Why had God asked him to make such a sacrifice! Abraham's heart was heavy, and for one whole night, he paced back and forth in his tent, wringing his hands and crying. But when morning came, he was calm. His great wisdom and faith told him that God must have a good reason for asking him to do this thing.

Abraham undertook at once to obey God's command. He took two young men with him and an ass laden with wood for the fire; and he went toward the mountain in the north, Isaac his son walking by his side.

Isaac was happy to be going on a trip with his father, and he laughed and joked along the way. Every time Isaac laughed Abraham felt a fierce pain in his heart, and he could hardly hold back the tears. But he pretended to be gay and he laughed hard at the jokes Isaac made.

For two days they walked, sleeping under the trees at night in the open country. And on the third day, Abraham saw the mountain far away. And as they drew near to the mountain, Abraham said to the young men:

"Stay here with the ass, while I go up yonder mountain with Isaac to worship; and when we have worshiped, we will come back to you."

Abraham took the wood for burning the sacrifice and gave it to his son Isaac, while he himself carried the fire and the knife. And the two went off together.

"Father!" said Isaac to Abraham.

"Yes, my son," he answered.

"Here are the fire and the wood," Isaac said, "but where is the lamb for the sacrifice?"

"God will Himself provide a lamb for the sacrifice, my son," said Abraham.

So they went both of them together.

When they came to the place of which God had told him, Abraham built the altar there, and laid the wood in order, and bound his son Isaac, and laid him upon the wood on the altar.

Then, with trembling hand, Abraham lifted his knife to kill Isaac . . . but lo and behold! Just at that moment, a great voice came out of the heavens calling,

"Abraham! Abraham!"

"Here am I!" answered Abraham. Then the voice said:

"Do not raise your hand against the boy, or do anything to him. For now I know that you fear God, since you have not withheld your son, your favored one, from Me."

Abraham joyfully cut away the cords that bound Isaac to the altar, and he hugged his son close and thanked God for sparing him.

Suddenly Isaac pointed to some bushes not far away.

"Look, father!" he cried. "There is the sacrifice!"

Through the happy tears in his eyes, Abraham saw a

ram, caught by his horns in the bushes. He took the ram and made a burnt offering of it to God, and God blessed Abraham for his great faith and sent him every good thing in life.

The place where this altar was built Abraham named Adonaijireh, words meaning, in the language that Abraham spoke, "The Lord will provide."

Abraham then went back to where his young men awaited him and Isaac, and they started together for Beersheba.

ISAAC AND REBEKAH

Sarah lived a hundred and twenty-seven years; and she died. Abraham buried her in the Cave of Machpelah in Hebron in the land of Canaan.

Isaac was now old enough to marry, and Abraham sought a wife for him; for in those countries the parents have always chosen the wives for their sons, and husbands for their daughters. Abraham did not want Isaac to marry a woman of the people in the land where he was living, for they were all worshipers of idols, and would not teach their children the ways of the Lord. For the same reason Abraham did not settle in one place, and build a city for himself and his people. By moving from place to place, Abraham kept his people apart.

But Abraham was old, and before he died, he wanted to make sure that his son, Isaac, had a good wife. You remember that when Abraham made his long journey to the land of Canaan, he stayed for a time at a place called Haran, in Mesopotamia. So he sent a trusted old servant, Eliezer, who had been in the family for many years, to his old homeland, to bring back a wife for Isaac.

And Eliezer took ten camels and many presents and went on the long journey. At last he came to the city where the family of Abraham was living. At the well, just outside of the city, in the evening, he made his camels kneel down. Then the servant prayed to the Lord that he would send him just the right young woman to be the wife of his master's son, Isaac:

"O Lord, the God of my master Abraham, give me success, I pray You, today, and deal kindly with my master, Abraham. Here I stand beside the well of water. The daughters of the townsmen come out to draw water. Let it come to pass that the maiden to whom I say, 'Pray lower your pitcher, that I may drink,' and who shall say, 'Drink, and I will give your camels also to drink,' may she be the maiden You have chosen for Your servant Isaac! Thereby shall I know that You have dealt kindly with my master."

Before he finished speaking, Rebekah came out, who was a daughter of Bethuel and the granddaughter of Nahor, Abraham's brother. She carried a pitcher upon her shoulder. The maiden was young and very beautiful. She went down to the well, and filled her pitcher; and as she came up, the servant, Eliezer, ran to meet her, and said:

"Let me drink, I beg you, a little water from your pitcher."

"Drink, sir," she said; and she quickly lowered the pitcher from her shoulder and gave him water to drink. When he had finished drinking she said:

"Let me draw water for your camels also, until they have enough."

She quickly emptied her pitcher into the trough and ran again to the well to draw some more water. She drew water for all his camels, while the man gazed upon her, eager to know whether the Lord had made his journey successful or not. When the camels finished drinking, Eliezer took a golden ring and two bracelets and gave them to her. Then he said:

"Whose daughter are you? Tell me I beg you. Is there room in your father's house for me to stay?"

"I am the daughter of Bethuel and the granddaughter of Nahor," she replied. "We have plenty of straw and feed, and there is room in which to lodge."

Eliezer bowed his head, and worshiped the Lord, saying:

"Blessed be the Lord, the God of my master Abraham! And as for me, the Lord has led me straight to the house of my master's brethren."

Rebekah ran swiftly to her father's house and told him that there was an old man outside, by the city well, who had offered her precious jewels for a drink of water. Her father, Bethuel, sent his son Laban out to bring the old man to the house. Eliezer told Laban he had an important message for his father, but Laban said that first they must give the camels food and water and that the old man must come in and wash his feet and rest. The old servant followed Laban to his father's house. The camels were fed and cared for and the old man gladly washed his weary feet. But he would not eat one bite of food until he had delivered Abraham's message to the father of the young girl who was to be Isaac's wife.

Laban took Eliezer to his father, who told him to speak.

"I am the servant of Abraham," he said, "and I have been sent by my master to seek a wife for his son, Isaac, in your land. My master told me that God would give me a sign so that I would know the right woman. And I asked God to let the right one offer water to my camels as well as to me. It was your daughter who was kind

enough to do this. In the name of my master, Abraham, I ask the hand of your daughter in marriage to my master's son, Isaac. It is God's will that this be so!"

The young woman's father said:

"Yes, I believe that it is God's will. Abraham is a wise and good man. His name is well-known throughout this land. I shall tell my daughter to prepare herself for the journey."

But the girl's mother was not quite so anxious for her beloved daughter to leave home, perhaps never to return.

"Please," she begged her husband, "let Rebekah speak for herself."

Rebekah came into the room, and her father told her what Abraham's servant had said. She stood with her eyes lowered.

"Well, my daughter," asked her father, "are you willing to go?"

Rebekah's heart was beating fast. The thought of a journey to a strange land filled her with excitement, but it was a rather frightening thought, too. She was silent a long time.

"Speak up, child!" cried her father.

Rebekah looked at her mother, whose eyes were filled with tears. Then she said softly, "Yes, father, I will go."

That night, as Rebekah lay under the desert stars, she snuggled farther down under her warm fur robe and wondered. She was very homesick and lonely, for in those days a journey took a long time, sometimes months, and Rebekah suddenly realized she might never see her parents or her brother again. But she wiped away her tears quickly and said a little prayer to God, asking him to give her courage and make her a good wife to the strange young man she was going to meet.

Several days later, Isaac was standing in a field, watch-

ing the sun set, when he saw camels in the distance, coming toward him. It was the old servant, Eliezer, returning with Rebekah. Rebekah noticed the young man standing in the field and she said to the servant:

"Who is that man?"

"That is Isaac, whom you are soon to marry," the old man answered.

A thousand thoughts chased themselves about in Rebekah's mind. What if the young man thought she was ugly! What if he didn't want her for his wife at all. What if, what if, what if . . . Rebekah was afraid she would burst into tears and the young man would think her very foolish, indeed. But she needn't have worried. For Isaac came running across the field and as soon as Rebekah saw him, she knew that he was good and kind, and certainly very handsome. But when Isaac said to his father's old servant, "Who is this?" Rebekah covered her face with a veil, which was the custom, until their marriage.

Then the old servant took Rebekah's soft hand and put it in Isaac's hand and said:

"This is Rebekah. I have brought her to be your wife."
When Isaac and Rebekah looked at each other, they both knew right away that it was indeed God's will for them to be together as long as they both should live.

JACOB AND ESAU

After Abraham died, his son Isaac lived in the land of Canaan. Like his father's home, Isaac's home was also a tent; and around him were the tents of his people, and many flocks of sheep and herds of cattle feeding wherever they could find grass to eat and water to drink, because these were so necessary in sheep raising.

This is the story of the twin brothers, Jacob and Esau, the sons of Isaac and Rebekah. Esau was just a few minutes older than his brother Jacob, and although these two brothers were twins, they were not exactly alike. Esau was very hairy. His hands and neck and arms were covered with thick, red hair, but Jacob's hands and neck were smooth. Esau grew up to be a strong man and he loved to hunt in the woods and mountains for deer. He would bring the deer home over his shoulder and lay it before his father, Isaac, and say:

"See, father, I have brought a deer and tonight I shall cook your favorite dish . . . venison . . . with my own special gravy and it will taste sweeter than the grapes in the vineyard!"

But Jacob was quiet and thoughtful, staying at home and caring for the flocks of his father.

Among the people in those lands, when a man died, his oldest son received twice as much as the younger of what the father owned and was the new head of the family. This was called his "birthright," for it was his right as the eldest born. So Esau, as the older, had a "birthright."

Jacob wanted very much to have the birthright which would come to Esau when his father died. Once, when Esau came home hungry and tired from hunting in the

fields, he saw that Jacob had a bowl of something that he had just cooked for dinner. And Esau said, "Give me some of that red stuff in the dish. Will you not give me some? I am hungry and feel faint."

Jacob said, "Sell me first your birthright."

And Esau answered:

"Here I am dying of hunger! What use is my birthright to me?"

Jacob said, "Swear to me first."

And Esau swore to him, and he sold his birthright to Jacob. And Jacob gave Esau bread and pottage of lentils. And Esau ate, and drank, and got up, and went his way. So Esau spurned his birthright.

Isaac became, at last, very old and feeble and so blind that he could scarcely see anything. One day he said to Esau:

"My son, I am very old and do not know how soon I must die. But before I die, I wish to give to you, my older son, God's blessing upon you and your children and your descendants. Go out into the fields, and with your bow and arrows shoot some animal that is good for food and

make me a dish of cooked meat, such as you know I love; and after I have eaten it, I will give you the blessing."

Esau went out into the fields to hunt, and find the kind of meat which his father liked the most.

Now Rebekah was listening, and heard all that Isaac had said to Esau. She felt that it would be better that Jacob should have the blessing instead of Esau; so she called to Jacob and told him what Isaac had told Esau, and she said:

"Now, my son, do what I tell you and you will get the blessing instead of your brother. Go to the flocks and bring me two little kids from the goats and I will cook them just like the meat which Esau cooks for your father. And you will bring it to your father; and he will think that you are Esau and will give you the blessing. You are the one who really deserves it."

But Jacob said, "You know that Esau and I are not alike. His neck and arms are covered with hair, while mine are smooth. My father will feel me, and he will discover that I am not Esau; and then, instead of giving me a blessing, I am afraid he will curse me."

But Rebekah answered her son, "Never mind, you do as I have told you. If any harm comes, it will come to me; so do not be afraid, but go and bring the meat."

Then Jacob went, and brought back a pair of little kids from the flock, and from them his mother made a dish of food, so that it would taste just as Isaac liked it. Then Rebekah found some of Esau's clothes, and dressed Jacob in them; and she placed on his neck and his hands some of the skins of the kids, so that his neck and hands would feel rough and hairy to the touch.

Then Jacob came into his father's tent, bringing the dinner and speaking as much like Esau as he could, he said:

"My father."

And Isaac said, "Here I am. Who are you, my son?"

And Jacob answered, "I am Esau, your oldest son. I have done as you bade me; now please sit up and eat the dinner that I have made; and then give me your blessing, as you promised."

And Isaac said, "How is it that you found it so quickly?"

Jacob answered, "Because the Lord your God showed me where to go."

Isaac did not feel certain that it was his son Esau, and he said, "Come nearer and let me feel you, so that I may know that you are really my son, Esau."

And Jacob went up close to Isaac's bed, and Isaac felt his face, and his neck, and his hands and he said:

"The voice sounds like Jacob, but the hands are the hands of Esau. Are you really my son Esau?"

And Jacob again said, "I am."

Then the old man ate the food that Jacob had brought

him, and he kissed Jacob, believing him to be Esau, and he gave him the blessing, saying to him:

"May God give you
Of the dew of heaven and the fat of the earth,
Abundance of new grain and wine.
Let peoples serve you,
And nations bow to you;
Be master over your brothers,
And let your mother's sons bow to you.
Cursed be they who curse you,
Blessed they who bless you."

As soon as Jacob had received the blessing, he rose up and hurried away. He had scarcely gone out, when Esau came in from his hunting, with the dish of food that he had cooked, and said:

"Let my father sit up and eat the food that I have brought and give me the blessing."

And Isaac said, "Why, who are you?"

Esau answered, "I am your son, your first-born son, Esau."

And Isaac trembled and said, "Who then is the one that came in and brought me food? And I have eaten his food and have blessed him; yes, and he shall be blessed."

When Esau heard this, he cried aloud, with a bitter cry, "O my father, my brother has taken away my blessing, just as he took away my birthright! But cannot you give me another blessing, too? Have you given everything to my brother?" And Isaac told him all that he had said to Jacob.

He said, "I have told him that he shall be the ruler, and that all his brothers and their children will be under him. I have promised him the richest ground for his crops and rains from heaven to make them grow. All these things have been spoken, and they must come to pass. What is left for me to promise you, my son?"

But Esau begged for another blessing, and Isaac said:

"My son, your dwelling shall be of the rich places of the earth and of the dew of heaven. You shall live by your sword, and your descendants shall serve his descendants. But there will come a time when you will break loose and be free of him."

All this came to pass many years afterward. The people who came from Esau lived in a land called Edom, on the south of the land of Israel, where Jacob's descendants lived. And after a time the Israelites became rulers over the Edomites; and later still the Edomites made themselves free from the Israelites. But all this took place hundreds of years after both Esau and Jacob had passed away. The blessing of God's covenant or promise came to Israel, and not to the people of Esau.

It was better that Jacob's descendants, those who came after him, should have the blessing, than that Esau's people should have had it; for Jacob's people worshiped God, and Esau's people walked in the way of the idols, and became wicked.

JACOB'S DREAM

How many times have you had a dream that seemed almost real? Sometimes it is a nightmare, and you are glad when you wake up to find that it isn't real, and you can snuggle down under the covers and go back to sleep.

This is the story of Jacob and his dream. Jacob, son of Isaac and Rebekah, was told to leave home by his mother, until his brother Esau would have forgiven him for having taken Esau's birthright.

She said to Jacob, "Before it is too late, go away from home and out of Esau's sight. Perhaps when Esau doesn't see you for a while he will forget his anger, and then you can come home again. Go and visit my brother Laban, your uncle, in Haran, and stay with him for a little while, until Esau's anger is past."

Jacob traveled all through the first day and, when the sun was low in the sky, he was very weary and decided to rest. He chose a place that was cool and grassy, but his pillow was a stone. However, Jacob was so weary that he fell asleep at once. About an hour after he fell asleep, he awoke with a start, for he thought someone had called his name. At first, Jacob forgot where he was, and thought he was at home in his own bed, but when his hand struck the hard stone, he remembered that he had left home, and he thought of his mother and father and his brother Esau. Perhaps he was not sure that he had been fair in his dealings with his brother.

"Here I lie in the lonely darkness, out in a field, with a stone for my pillow. I am far away from the home where I played as a child, and where my brother Esau and I grew up together!"

Then Jacob sighed with homesickness, and lay down once more on his bed of grass and his pillow of stone, and gazed up at the bright stars.

"How bright the stars are," he thought. "The angels have lighted all their lamps to cheer me on this lonely night!"

Then he fell asleep once more, and dreamed. In his sleep he saw a mighty ladder, so long that it reached from the earth clear up into heaven. And hundreds of angels were going up and down the ladder. Never had Jacob seen such beings. They wore long robes that seemed to be woven out of some kind of mist, and the faces of the angels were so beautiful and bright that Jacob was almost blinded, and had to rub his eyes. Just then, he was startled to hear a voice; it was the voice of God Who stood beside him and said:

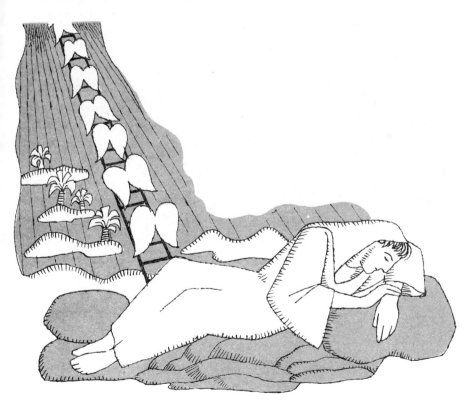

"I am the LORD, the God of your father Abraham and the God of Isaac: the ground on which you are lying I will give to you and to your offspring. Your descendants shall be as the dust of the earth; you shall spread out to the west and to the east, to the north and to the south. All the families of the earth shall bless themselves by you and your descendants. Remember, I am with you: I will protect you wherever you go and will bring you back to this land. I will not leave you until I have done what I have promised you."

Then the voice was quiet, and Jacob jumped up from the ground. He ran toward the wonderful ladder, thinking if he could climb it himself, he would look upon the face of God. But when he reached out his hand to touch the ladder, it faded away like mist, and Jacob stood rubbing his eyes and looking all around him. Where were the beautiful angels? They, too, were gone. Jacob gazed up into the sky, but only the silent stars looked back at him. Then he realized that he had had a wonderful dream, in which the voice of God had spoken to him.

"Oh, God," he cried aloud, "I know now that You will bless me on my journey, and that you will bring me back here to this very land, and it will be my own. And I shall go once again to my father's house in peace."

Then Jacob took the stone which he had used for a pillow and set it in the ground, and poured oil over it and made it an altar to God. Jacob called the place Beth-el which means the House of God.

JACOB AND RACHEL

After Jacob's dream about the ladder, he felt strong and ready to go on with his journey eastward, to the land where his uncle lived.

As he was crossing a field, he saw a well, with a great stone over it. Beside the well were some shepherds and their sheep. Jacob said to the men:

"Do you know a man called Laban, the grandson of Nahor?"

"Yes," answered the men, "we know him well. Look, here comes Laban's daughter Rachel, with her father's sheep."

"But it is not time to water the sheep," said Jacob, "it is still early in the day."

"But the stone is so heavy," answered the shepherds, "that we must wait until all the flocks are gathered here. Then we all have to push on the stone to move it away from the mouth of the well."

Just then, Rachel came up to the well. When Jacob looked at her, he saw that she was very beautiful, and he loved her at once. Jacob was very strong, he walked up to the great stone over the mouth of the well and with one mighty push, he sent it rolling to one side. Then the shepherds let their sheep drink, and Jacob led Rachel's sheep to the well. He told her that he was the son of her father's sister, Rebekah.

Rachel ran to tell her father the good news.

"Father, father," she cried, "Jacob, your sister's son, has come all the way from his home to visit us. He is waiting by the well."

Laban was very pleased. He went out to meet Jacob and brought him to his house. Jacob helped Laban in the fields, and helped tend the sheep.

Now Laban had two daughters: Leah, the older, and Rachel, the younger. Leah had a very sweet face, but

Rachel was far more beautiful and Jacob had loved her from the first moment he saw her by the well.

Jacob said to Laban, "If you will give me the hand of your daughter Rachel in marriage, I will serve you for seven years."

Laban agreed, and for seven years Jacob served Rachel's father. It was the custom then for the elder daughter to be married first, and often the younger girl had to wait for her sister to get a husband. And so, after the seven years had passed, when Jacob said to Laban:

"Now it is time for Rachel to become my wife!"

Laban gathered together all the people, and a great feast was set before them. There was much merrymaking. Then Laban brought in the bride, with a heavy veil over her face. After she and Jacob were married, the bride lifted the veil and Jacob was shocked to see that he had married, not Rachel, but Leah, her older sister!

Jacob was very angry. He went to Laban and said:

"Why have you tricked me like this! It was Rachel you promised me after seven years of hard work, not Leah!"

But Laban said:

"In my country, the older sister must be given in marriage before the younger sister! Serve me seven years more and I will give you Rachel also for your wife." For it was the law in those days that a man could have more than one wife.

Jacob loved Rachel so much he agreed to work still another seven years.

As the years passed, Jacob began to long to see his old home, and he wanted to meet his brother Esau again, and make friends with him. Jacob went to Laban, who was now an old man, and said:

"I want to take my wives and children and go back to my homeland."

But Laban begged Jacob to stay with him.

"Since you came to my house, the Lord has blessed me, and given me many cattle and sheep. What shall I give you so that you will stay here and serve me?"

"Give me all the sheep and cattle that are born speckled or spotted," answered Jacob. Laban agreed to do this, because there were not many speckled or spotted cattle or sheep. But God knew that Laban had tricked Jacob many times and treated him badly. God blessed Jacob and caused many sheep and cows to be born speckled and spotted. Soon Jacob owned more sheep and cattle than Laban did. Laban was jealous and angry and said unkind things to Jacob.

Jacob was very unhappy. He prayed to God for help. God said:

"Take your family and servants and flocks and go back to your homeland. I will bless you and see that no harm comes to you."

Jacob was very happy when he heard these words. He thanked God for helping and blessing him. Then, with a heart full of joy, he went to tell his wife Rachel and his wife Leah to prepare to begin the journey back to the land of Canaan.

JACOB WRESTLES WITH AN ANGEL

As Jacob and his family and servants came close to Canaan, Jacob sent messengers ahead to tell his brother Esau that he was coming back home. But when the messengers returned, they said to Jacob:

"We told your brother Esau that you are returning home with plenty of sheep and cattle and with your wives and children. Your brother Esau is on his way to meet you, and he is bringing four hundred men with him!"

Then Jacob was afraid. He thought Esau was still angry with him and was coming to seize his cattle and sheep and attack his servants and family. So Jacob divided his flocks and servants into two groups.

"If Esau captures one group," he said, "the other group will escape."

Then Jacob went off by himself to a quiet place and knelt to pray.

"Save me, God, from my brother's anger," he said. "You promised me when I left my homeland that no harm would befall me. Please keep your promise to me now. I know I am not worthy of all the blessings you have given me. Spare me and my wives and children from Esau's wrath!"

Then Jacob took his finest sheep and goats and said to his servants:

"Take these to my brother as a gift. Tell him I am coming to meet him."

That night, while he was waiting alone for the day to dawn, Jacob suddenly felt himself seized by a pair of strong arms, and he found himself wrestling with a strange man. Jacob and the man wrestled all through the night. Then, just as the first rays of the sun peeped over

the hills, the stranger said, "Let me go!" But Jacob fought on. Then the man put his hand in the hollow of Jacob's thigh, and suddenly Jacob could not move his leg, for it was out of joint. Then he knew this stranger was an angel of the Lord, sent to try his strength.

And the angel said: "Let me go, for the day is breaking."

And Jacob said: "I will not let you go until you bless me." And the angel said:

"What is your name?"

And Jacob answered, "Jacob is my name."

Then the angel said:

"Your name shall no more be called Jacob, but Israel, that is, 'He who wrestles with God.' For you have wrestled with God and with men, and you have won."

And the angel blessed him there. And the sun rose as the angel left him; and Jacob gave a name to that place. He called it Peniel which, in the language that Jacob

spoke, means "The face of God." "For," said Jacob, "I have met God face to face." And after this Jacob was lame for, in wrestling, he had strained his thigh.

And as Jacob went across the brook Jabbok, early in the morning, he looked up, and there was Esau before him. He bowed with his face to the ground, over and over again, as people do in those lands when they meet someone of higher rank than their own. But Esau ran to meet him and placed his arms around his neck and kissed him; and the two brothers wept together. All their old quarrels were forgotten in the joy of seeing each other once more. And so after many trials, Jacob, now called Israel, returned to the Land of Canaan.

Not long afterward the aged Isaac died, and his sons, Jacob and Esau, buried him in the cave at Hebron where Abraham and Sarah were already buried. Esau with his children and his cattle went away to a land on the southeast of Canaan, which was called Edom. And Jacob, or Israel, and his family lived in the land of Canaan, dwelling in tents and moving from place to place wherever they could find good pasture for their flocks.

After Jacob came back to the land of Canaan with his eleven sons, another son was born to him, the second child of Rachel, whom Jacob loved so well. Soon after the baby was born, Rachel died, and Jacob was filled with sorrow. Jacob named his youngest child Benjamin. Now Jacob had twelve sons. Most of them were grown-up men, but Joseph was a boy, seventeen years old, and his brother Benjamin was just a baby.

JOSEPH'S COAT OF MANY COLORS

Joseph was very brave and had many exciting adventures, even when he was a very young boy. Jacob loved Joseph more than any of his other sons because there was something about Joseph that set him apart from the others. Somehow, Joseph had the mark of a leader, and his father was very proud of him. He would put his hand on Joseph's curly hair and say:

"Ah, my son, some day you will be a great man. Your old father can tell this, just by the proud way you walk and the quick way you learn your lessons."

Joseph's brothers were very jealous of him, and Joseph, by his boasting and proud ways, did nothing to make them feel differently. Jacob was especially proud of Joseph's good looks, and one day he called Joseph to him and said:

"See, my son, here is a coat. What do you think of it?"

Joseph gazed in wonder at the coat his father was holding.

"Oh, father, it is beautiful! It is like a rainbow woven into cloth. Surely it must belong to a king, it is so rich and elegant!"

Jacob smiled and held the coat for Joseph to try.

Joseph walked back and forth, admiring it, and rubbing his hand gently over the fine cloth.

"Father," he said, "if I were a king, I would have a coat like this for my very own!"

His father laughed and said:

"Then you are a king, my son, for the coat is yours! It is my special gift to you. God bless you, and may you wear the coat for many happy years."

Joseph was so proud of his coat that he wore it every day. At night, he put it close to his bed. But his brothers were even more jealous when they saw the coat. It was the kind of coat that chiefs wore.

"He struts about like a foolish peacock in his coat of many colors!" cried one brother.

"He may look like a peacock, but he acts like a silly goose!" said another.

Joseph's brothers became so jealous of him that they could not speak a kind word to him, and Joseph was very lonely at times. One day, he told them something that made them hate him even more. It was about that time that Joseph had dreamed a strange dream.

"I dreamed that we were binding sheaves in the field," he said to his brothers, "and my sheaf suddenly rose up and your sheaves all bowed down to it as if it were a king!"

Then his brothers became very angry indeed, and cried out to Joseph:

"Hear the bold fellow! And do you suppose that some day you shall rule over us and we shall be your slaves! You'd better hold your tongue!"

But a few days later, Joseph dreamed another dream.

"What a strange dream I had last night," he said to his brothers one morning. "I dreamed that the sun and the moon and eleven stars all bowed down to me as if I were a king!"

Now Joseph's father overheard him tell his brothers about this dream, and he knew the brothers were already so jealous they could hardly speak to Joseph. He knew

this story about the second dream would anger them even more. And he even thought that Joseph might be making up stories about these wonderful dreams.

"Joseph," he cried, "if you are telling us stories about these dreams just to startle us, stop your foolishness at once. Do you mean to tell me that even your mother and father will one day bow down to you like servants?"

You see, in those far off days dreams were thought to be very important, and people were always trying to figure out their meanings. Joseph's father thought the sun and moon represented him and Joseph's mother, and that the eleven stars were Joseph's eleven brothers.

But Joseph looked straight into his father's eyes and Jacob could tell his son was telling the truth.

"Oh, no, father," said Joseph. "I am only telling you what I dreamed last night. It seemed so strange. First the sheaves of grain, bowing to my sheaf. Then the sun, the moon, and the eleven stars bowing down to me. What can it mean, father?"

"It was just a dream, son," said his father. "You have been walking about in your coat of many colors and pretending you are a king! It is natural for you to have such a dream, with such thoughts in your head. You had better go out into the fields and forget these foolish dreams that mean nothing!"

But Jacob wondered about Joseph's two dreams, even though he pretended that he did not think they meant anything.

JOSEPH SOLD INTO SLAVERY

Once, when Joseph's ten older brothers were taking care of the flock in the fields near Shechem, nearly fifty miles from Hebron where Jacob's tents were spread, Jacob wished to send a message to his sons.

He called Joseph and said to him, "Your brothers are near Shechem with the flocks. Go to them and find out if they are well, and if the flocks are doing well; then bring me word."

Joseph was seventeen years old, and Jacob knew that he could trust him to go alone over the country, and find his way for fifty miles, and back home again; so he went forth on his journey, walking northward over the mountains.

When Joseph reached Shechem, he could not find his brothers, for they had taken their flocks to another place. A man met Joseph wandering in the field and asked him, "Whom are you seeking?" Joseph said, "I am looking for my brothers, the sons of Jacob. Can you tell me where I will find them?" And the man said, "They are at Dothan, for I heard them say that they were going there." Then Joseph walked over the hills to Dothan, which was fifteen miles farther. And his brothers saw him from afar coming toward them. They knew him by his bright garment; and one said to another:

"Here he comes. Let us kill him quickly and throw his body into a pit. We can tell father a wild beast devoured him."

"Yes, yes!" cried the other brothers, "and then we'll see how soon we bow down to this smart young fellow who dreams he is a king and we are his servants!"

But Joseph's brother Reuben was more kindhearted than the others, and he could not bear to see young Joseph killed.

"Wait!" he cried. "Do not kill him. Throw him into the pit, and let us not have our own brother's blood upon our hands!"

When Joseph came running up to his brothers, happy to have found them, they seized him, tore his beautiful coat off his back, and threw him into a deep pit, where there was no food or water. Joseph cried out to his brothers, but they turned away and left him. They sat down to eat before starting out again, and while they were eating, Judah, one of the brothers, pointed to the

distant hills, where a caravan of camels could be seen.

"Look," he said, "it is a caravan of Ishmaelites carrying spices, medicines, and perfumes on their way to Egypt! What do we gain by killing our brother and covering up his blood? Come, let us sell him to the Ishmaelites, but let us not do away with him ourselves. After all, he is our brother, our own flesh."

His brothers agreed. They drew him out of the pit, and they sold him as a slave to the Ishmaelites who were on their way to Egypt with their caravan. The Ishmaelites paid twenty pieces of silver for Joseph, who had once dreamed he was a king!

Reuben, the eldest, who felt more responsible for Joseph than the others, was not with them when Joseph was sold. When he returned, he went to the pit, thinking he would take Joseph out and send him home to his father. When he saw that the pit was empty, he cried out:

"He is not there! Joseph is not in the pit. He is gone!"

Then the brothers became frightened at what they had done. They killed a young goat and dipped Joseph's coat

into the goat's blood. Then they returned home and showed Jacob the beautiful coat of many colors, now torn and dirty and spotted with the blood of a goat.

"See, father," they cried out, "we have found this coat. But we have not found Joseph! We do not know if this is Joseph's coat or not. Can you tell?"

How could poor old Jacob mistake the wonderful coat he had given the son he loved so dearly? There was no other coat like it in all the land. The old man took the coat and cried over it.

"Joseph, my son, my dearest little son," he kept saying over and over. His sons felt guilty when they saw how terribly grieved their father was. But it was too late now to bring Joseph back. Jacob mourned his son Joseph for many days, and soon the coat became spotted with the tears Jacob wept for the son he thought was dead.

JOSEPH IN EGYPT

The men who bought Joseph from his brothers were called Ishmaelites, because they belonged to the family of Ishmael, who, you remember, was the son of Hagar, the servant of Sarah. Now let us see what happened to Joseph, after he was sold to the Ishmaelites and taken to Egypt.

Imagine how Joseph must have felt, riding along on a donkey, every mile taking him farther and farther away from his home and his old father. His own brothers had left him to die in the deep pit!

"They would have been kinder to have killed me," thought Joseph to himself bitterly. "It would have been better than starving to death or dying of thirst."

Joseph rode along with the caravan. His body was weary and sore from having been thrown down into the hard rocky pit. He was half asleep with weariness when one of the men in the caravan prodded him roughly and cried:

"Come, you lazy beggar, we are resting for tonight. Come help us feed and water the animals."

After Joseph had done this, he was given a crust of bread and some water. Just then, he happened to glance up at the sky. The sun was going down and the desert sky was gold and pale green and crimson, and the mountains in the distance were a deep purple.

"Many colors," whispered Joseph to himself, "just like my beautiful coat of many colors! Oh God," he cried, "please let my father find me some day!"

"So!" cried a harsh voice. "Our food is not good enough

for this high and mighty beggar!" It was one of the men who saw that Joseph dropped his bread. He gave Joseph a kick that sent him sprawling across the ground. Joseph lay where he had fallen. He was too weary to get up. He slept there all night, and in the morning the caravan moved on toward Egypt.

How strange it must have seemed to the boy who had lived in tents to see the great river Nile and the cities, thronged with people, and the temples, and the mighty pyramids!

When the caravan reached Egypt, Joseph was sold again, this time to a man named Potiphar, who was one of the Pharaoh's officers. The kings of Egypt of that time were called Pharaohs. Now Joseph did not complain or whine about what had happened to him. He made up his mind to do the best he could, and put all his faith and trust in God's help. He served his master Potiphar well. Potiphar saw how hard Joseph worked and how honest he was, and he made Joseph the manager of his fields and of all his household. Potiphar's affairs went well in the hands of this intelligent young Hebrew. But Joseph's troubles were just beginning.

Joseph was very handsome, and Potiphar's wife fell in love with him. But Joseph was loyal to his beliefs and to his master, and would have nothing to do with her. She became very angry that a man who had once been a lowly slave should show such disdain for the mistress of the house. Potiphar's wife began to make up stories about Joseph and tell them to her husband, poisoning his mind against Joseph. At last, Potiphar became very angry and had Joseph thrown into prison.

You would think that Joseph would have felt very bitter by this time. First his brothers had turned against him, and now this man whom he had served so well had ordered him thrown into prison for something he had not even done. But the one thing that kept Joseph from losing his courage was his strong faith in God. Even in the dark and gloomy prison, he prayed to God; and God was with him, and heard his prayers. God answers faithful prayers like Joseph's, as you will soon see.

Once more, Joseph worked hard. He was so well-behaved in the prison that the keeper put him in charge of all the other prisoners. Joseph spent many hours cheering up these poor men. Prisons in those days were damp, dark dungeons, and the prisoners were fed very little, and only the very worst kind of food, some of it spoiled and rotten and not fit to eat.

But Joseph kept his mind on the day when God would send him help. He kept thinking of the good things there were in life. At night, as he lay on the hard stone floor of the prison, he would think of his father. He would look at the few stars he could see through the bars across the window and he would think of how beautiful these stars were and how great was the God who created them. These thoughts kept Joseph from dying in the prison. He refused to give up hope.

THE BAKER AND THE BUTLER

One day, two men were brought into the prison; one was the Pharaoh's chief baker, the other his head butler. These men had offended their king and he had become angry with them and ordered them sent to prison where they were put in Joseph's care. One morning, Joseph noticed that the butler and the baker seemed very sad.

"Why do you look so troubled?" he asked kindly.

"It is the dream I had last night," said the butler. "I wish there were someone here who could tell me what it means."

Joseph smiled.

"I was a dreamer myself once," he said. "Tell me your dream. I shall try to tell you its meaning."

"I dreamed of a grape vine," said the butler. "It had three branches and I saw them blossom and bear fruit before my very eyes, and Pharaoh's cup was in my hand, and I pressed the juice of the grapes into the cup and gave the cup to Pharaoh."

"I shall tell you what this dream means," said Joseph thoughtfully. "The three branches are three days. Within three days Pharaoh shall restore you to your place as his butler. But remember me when this happens. Tell Pharaoh that I am a Hebrew who was brought here unjustly as a slave and perhaps he will take pity on me."

Then Joseph turned to the king's baker, who said:

"I dreamed I had three white baskets on my head, and in the uppermost basket there were all kinds of cakes and meats for Pharaoh, and the birds ate them out of the basket."

Joseph looked very sad; then he said:

"Poor man! The three baskets are three days. In three days, Pharaoh shall hang you from a tree and the birds shall eat your flesh!"

Three days after this, the keeper of the prison came to tell the butler and the baker that Pharaoh wanted to see them. When they were taken into Pharaoh's presence, he restored the butler to his old place, but he told the baker he would be hanged from a tree. Joseph had been right about the dreams. But the butler forgot all about Joseph and never mentioned his name to the Pharaoh.

Joseph remained in the prison for two more long, dreary years. He kept praying, but he had almost given up hope,

when one day the keeper unlocked the iron door and told him he was to see the great Pharaoh himself. The Pharaoh had dreamed a dream which greatly troubled him. He had called all the magicians and wise men of his court to tell him what the dreams meant. But he was not satisfied with what they told him.

Then suddenly the chief butler, who was by the king's table, remembered his own dream in the prison two years before, and remembered, too, the young man who had explained its meaning so exactly. And he said:

"I apologize for my faults today. Two years ago Pharaoh was angry with his servants, with me and the chief baker, and he sent us to prison. While we were in prison, one night each of us dreamed a dream, and the next day a young man in the prison, a Hebrew from the land of Canaan, told us what our dreams meant; and in three days they came true, just as the Hebrew had said. I think that if this young man is still in the prison, he could tell the king the meaning of his dreams."

You notice that the butler spoke of Joseph as "a Hebrew." The people of Israel, to whom Joseph belonged, were called Hebrews as well as Israelites. The word Hebrew means "one who crosses over," and was given to the Israelites because Abraham, their father, had come from a land on the other side of the river Euphrates, and had crossed over the river on his way to Canaan. Hebrews were not slaves in those days.

Then Pharaoh sent in haste to the prison for Joseph; and Joseph was taken out, and he was dressed in new garments and was led in to Pharaoh in the palace. And Pharaoh said to Joseph, "I have dreamed a dream, and there is no one who can tell what it means. And I have been told that you have power to understand dreams and what they mean."

And Joseph answered Pharaoh, "The power is not in me; but God will give Pharaoh a good answer. What is the dream that the king has dreamed?"

"In my dream, I stood by the river and seven fat cows came out of the river and they fed in a meadow. Then seven more cows came up after them, but they were skinny and ill-fed, such as I never saw in Egypt, and they stood beside the other cows and ate them up. And after having eaten them up, they were as skinny and ugly as before. Then I woke up, and when I fell asleep again, I had another dream. In the second dream I saw seven fat ears of corn; then seven thin, withered ears sprang up beside them and the seven thin ears ate up the seven fat ears."

Joseph said to the mighty Pharaoh:

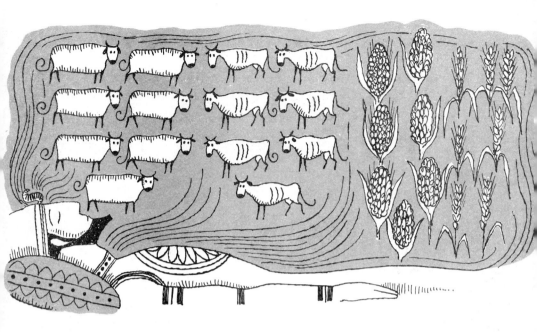

"I shall tell you what God puts into my mind to say, for God is the only one who knows the meanings of dreams. Both your dreams are really the same. The seven cows and the seven ears of corn are seven years. The seven fat cows and the seven good ears of corn are seven good years, and the seven lean cows and the seven empty ears of corn are seven years of famine. Egypt shall have seven rich years, but they will be followed by seven years of terrible famine, when the grain shall wither in the fields. You must set a wise man over Egypt who will store up grain in great storehouses so that when the famine comes there will be food for the people to eat."

Pharaoh looked at Joseph for a long time. Then he said:

"Since you are so wise, and your God has shown you such wisdom, you surely must be the right man to do this thing. I command you to take charge of collecting and storing the grain. Indeed, I shall give you the highest office in the land. Only I, Pharaoh, shall be above you."

And Pharaoh took from his own hand the ring which held his seal, and put it on Joseph's hand, so that he could sign for the king with the seal, in the king's place. And he dressed Joseph in robes of fine linen, and put around his neck a gold chain. And he made Joseph ride in a chariot which was next in rank to his own. And servants cried out before Joseph, "Bend the knee." And Pharaoh gave him an Egyptian noblewoman as his wife, and she bore him two sons. Thus Joseph was ruler over all the land of Egypt.

So the slave boy, who was sent to prison without deserving it, came out of prison to be a prince and a master over all the land. You see that God had not forgotten Joseph, even when he seemed to have left him to suffer alone.

JOSEPH MEETS HIS BROTHERS

We have seen how Joseph, son of Jacob, became the ruler of all Egypt, second in command only to the mighty Pharaoh himself. Joseph was right about Pharaoh's dreams, and after seven good years, there came seven years of terrible famine. People were dying of starvation everywhere, but not in Egypt. For Joseph had wisely stored much grain during the seven good years, and when Pharaoh saw that Joseph had told him the true meaning of his dreams, he respected him more than ever.

But what of Joseph's father and his eleven brothers? The famine was so great that it had spread over many countries, and even into the land of Canaan where Jacob and his sons lived. Jacob was quite old now and he was worried when he saw that there would be little food to eat. He said to his sons:

"I have heard that there is much corn in Egypt. Go down into Egypt and take money to buy corn, so that we shall not starve."

All Joseph's brothers, except for Benjamin, made ready to make the journey to Egypt. Jacob would not let Benjamin go with them for, next to Joseph, Benjamin was his most beloved son, and he well remembered the son who had left home long ago and never returned.

Now when Joseph's brothers reached Egypt, they were directed to Joseph's great house. You must remember that it had been many years since they had last seen their brother. Joseph had been just a lad when they threw him into the pit. Now he was a man, and he was dressed in Egyptian clothes and spoke the Egyptian language. When Joseph saw his brothers walk into the room, he recognized them at once.

His brothers did not recognize this great Egyptian lord as the young brother they had almost left to die in a pit so many years ago. There was a man present while Joseph bargained with his brothers, who translated the languages so that Joseph and his brothers could understand each other, for Joseph pretended that he did not know the language his brothers were speaking. The man who translated was called an interpreter.

The brothers bowed low as soon as they came before

Joseph. Joseph remembered the dreams he had had when he was a young boy. His brothers' sheaves of grain had bowed down to his sheaf. The sun, moon, and eleven stars had bowed to him.

"Strange, strange," he whispered to himself. "So many years have passed since I dreamed those dreams. Yet, today they have come true!"

After the brothers had told Joseph that they wanted corn and had money to pay for it, Joseph took a deep breath and then he said:

"I do not believe you are honest men who have come here just to buy corn! I know what you have come for. You have come as spies, to see how helpless the land is, so that you can bring an army against us and make war on us."

They were amazed and said:

"Oh, no, my lord. We aren't spies. We are brothers who have come to buy food for ourselves, our father and youngest brother at home."

"You say you are the sons of one man, who is your father? Is he living?" asked Joseph. "Tell me all about yourselves."

And they said, "Our father is an old man in Canaan. We did have a younger brother, but he was lost; and we have one brother still, who is the youngest of all, but his father could not spare him to come with us."

"No," said Joseph roughly, testing them, "you are not good, honest men. You are spies. I shall put you all in prison, except one of you; and he shall go and bring that youngest brother of yours; and when I see him, then I will believe that you have told the truth."

So Joseph put all ten men in prison and kept them under guard for three days; then he sent for them again.

Then he turned again to them and spoke roughly as before, and said:

"This I will do, for I serve God: I will let you all go home, except one man. One of you I will shut up in prison; but the rest of you can go home and take food for your people. And you must come back and bring your youngest brother with you, and I shall know then that you have spoken the truth."

They did not know that he could understand their language and they said to each other, while Joseph pretended not to hear:

"This has come upon us because of the wrong that we did to our brother Joseph, more than twenty years ago. We heard him cry and plead with us when we threw him into the pit, and we would not have mercy on him. God is giving us only what we deserve."

And their brother Reuben cried out to them:

"Remember, I told you not to sin against the child but you would not listen!"

When Joseph heard this, he could not hold back his tears. He left the room and wept, for he longed to tell his brothers who he was. The sight of their familiar faces brought back all the memories of his childhood and his old home.

Then Joseph gave orders, and his servants seized his brother Simeon, and took him away to prison.

Then he told his servants to fill the brothers' sacks with corn, but he also had the servants secretly put back into each sack the money the brothers had brought to pay for the grain.

Joseph's brothers took their sacks of corn and returned to their home. But when they opened the sacks and Jacob saw the money on top of the grain, and they told him about Simeon, he cried aloud:

"Why have these things happened to an old man like me! First my son Joseph was devoured by wild beasts. Now Simeon is held prisoner in Egypt, and is already probably dead! And now this Egyptian wants my beloved Benjamin also. I tell you it shall not be! I would rather starve than send Benjamin to such a man."

JOSEPH REVEALS HIMSELF

The famine became worse as each day passed. Finally, one day, Jacob's son Judah came to him and said:

"Father, my children are hungry. We are all going to die unless we get food. Send Benjamin with me, and I will take care of him. I promise you that I will bring him safely home. If he does not come back, let me bear the blame forever. He must go or we shall die for want of food; and we might have been to Egypt and come home again, if we had not been kept back."

Jacob sighed deeply and bowed his head.

"Very well," he said. "Take Benjamin and go. And take with you double the money, carrying back with you the money that was replaced in the mouths of your bags; perhaps it was a mistake."

With a heavy heart, old Jacob watched Benjamin ride away with his brothers.

When Joseph saw Benjamin, his younger brother, the child of his own mother, Rachel, he said, "Is this your youngest brother, of whom you spoke to me? God be gracious unto you, my son."

Joseph ordered the table to be set for dinner. They set

Joseph's table for him alone, as the ruler, and another table for his Egyptian officers, and another for the eleven men from Canaan; for Joseph had brought Simeon out of prison and had given him a place with his brothers.

Then Joseph commanded his servants to fill his brothers' sacks once more with grain, but he also whispered to them to put the money for the grain into the sacks, just as they had done before. Then Joseph told one of his servants to hide his own silver cup in Benjamin's sack.

Joseph's brothers thanked him for his kindness and set out for home once more. As soon as the brothers were out of sight, Joseph said to his servants:

"Go, and overtake those men. And say to them, 'Why have you returned evil for good?' "

When the brothers saw the servants riding up behind them, they wondered what they had done wrong. The servants ordered them to throw their sacks of corn on the

ground, and each sack was opened. When the silver cup rolled out of Benjamin's sack, the young man cried out in alarm:

"Look, it is a silver cup! But how did it get into my sack? I did not put it there!"

Joseph's servants just laughed at Benjamin and shoved him roughly back on his donkey. They ordered all the brothers to come back with him to Joseph's palace.

Joseph was awaiting them, and when the brothers bowed before him, his brother Judah cried:

"My lord, what can we say to you? We know not how this silver cup got into our brother's sack. Have mercy on us!"

But Joseph said sternly:

"Take your grain and return to your father. But the man in whose sack the cup was found shall remain with me and be my servant."

Then Judah cried out in alarm:

"Oh, my lord, we cannot return home without Benjamin! Our father grieved many years for his other son, Joseph. Benjamin is like the sun and moon and stars to him. I pray you do not do this thing to an old man, for our father said to us before we left home, 'If harm shall come to Benjamin, you will bring sorrow to an old man and bow him down with sadness!' Let me stay instead of Benjamin."

Joseph could not keep pretending any longer when he heard these words, for he knew how many years his old father had been grieving, and he could not bear to bring him any more suffering. He began to weep, and he cried out to his brothers:

"Do you not recognize me, my brothers? I am Joseph whom you sold into slavery!"

The brothers could scarcely believe they had heard

right. Then when they finally realized that this great Egyptian lord was really their long-lost brother Joseph, they were afraid. But Joseph said to them:

"Do not fear. I shall not punish you for your sin against me. Don't you see, it was God's will that I come here to Egypt and store up corn so that we all might eat in the time of the famine. But come, make haste to bring my father to me, for I am very anxious to see him!"

Pharaoh was pleased to see Joseph's family and said:

"Let your father, and your brothers and their households come to the land of Egypt, and I will give them good land to live on, and they shall be rich."

Can you imagine Jacob's surprise and joy when the brothers returned home and told him that the Egyptian lord was his own son Joseph! At first the old man did not believe them, but when they showed him the donkeys and the grain and the gifts, Jacob wept and thanked God for keeping Joseph alive all those years.

They came down to Egypt, Jacob and sixty-six of his children and grandchildren. Joseph rode in his chariot to meet his father, and fell on his neck and wept, and Jacob said, "Now I am ready to die, since I know that you are still

alive; and I have seen your face." And Joseph brought
his father in to see the Pharaoh; and Jacob, as an old
man, gave his blessing to the king.

The part of the land of Egypt that Joseph found for his
brothers to make their home was called Goshen. It was on
the east, between Egypt and the desert, and it was a very
rich land, where the soil gave large harvests and there
was rich pasture for their flocks. But at that time, and for
five years after, there were no crops, because of the famine
that was in the land. During those years, the people of
Israel in the land of Goshen were fed as were all the
people of Egypt, with grain from the storehouses of
Joseph.

Jacob lived to be one hundred and forty-seven years
old. Before he died, he addressed Joseph and all his sons
and said to them:

"When I die, do not bury me in the land of Egypt, but

take my body to the land of Canaan, and bury me in the cave at Hebron, with Abraham and Isaac, my father."

And Joseph brought his two sons, Manasseh and Ephraim, to his father's bed. Jacob's eyes were dim with age, as his father Isaac's had been, and he could not see the two young men. And he said, "Who are these?"

And Joseph said, "They are my two sons, whom God has given me in this land."

"Bring them to me," said Jacob, "that I may bless them before I die. I never expected to see you again—and now I see your children, too!"

Jacob blessed Joseph and his two sons saying:

"The God in whose ways my fathers Abraham and
    Isaac walked,
The God who has been my shepherd from my birth to
    this day—
The Angel who has redeemed me from all harm—
Bless the lads.
And may they be teeming multitudes upon the earth."

He then called all his sons to his bedside and gave each one a special blessing, foretelling the future and destiny of each and every one of them.

When Jacob died, a great funeral was held. They carried his body up out of Egypt to the land of Canaan, and buried it—as he had said to them—in the cave of Machpelah, where Abraham and Isaac were buried already.

After this Joseph lived to a good old age, until he was a hundred and ten years old. Before he died, he said to his children and to all the children of Israel, who had now increased to very many people:

"I am going to die; but God will come to you and will bring you up out of this land, into your own land, which he promised to your fathers, to Abraham and Isaac and Jacob. When I die, do not bury me in Egypt, but keep my body until you go out of this land, and take it with you."

So when Joseph died, they embalmed his body as the Egyptians embalmed the bodies of their kings and great men. They filled it with drugs and spices, so that it would not decay; and they placed his body in a stone coffin and kept it in the land of Goshen among the people of Israel. Thus Joseph not only showed his faith in God's promise, that he would bring his people back to the land of Canaan; but he also encouraged the faith of those who came after him.

THE BABY IN THE BASKET BOAT

As long as Joseph lived, and for some time after, the people of Israel were treated kindly by the Egyptians, out of their love for Joseph, who had saved Egypt from suffering by famine. But after a long time, another Pharaoh began to rule over Egypt, who cared nothing for Joseph or Joseph's people. When he saw how the Hebrews were multiplying and prospering, he was afraid they would seize the throne one day and rule all Egypt. Now the Hebrews had no such thought at all. In fact, they were hoping that some day a great leader would come and lead them to the land that God had promised Abraham and Isaac and Jacob.

The wicked Pharaoh tried every trick he could think of to weaken the Hebrews. He made slaves of them and gave them all the hard work to do, like working in the fields, and carrying brick and stone for building houses and the pyramids. When the Hebrews fell down with weariness, the taskmasters, cruel men with whips, would beat them to make them get up again and work. But God was with the Hebrews, as He is with all good people who are unjustly treated. Instead of dying the Hebrews grew stronger and stronger.

Then one wicked Pharaoh thought of a plan he was sure would put an end to the Hebrews once and for all times. He ordered that all the boy babies born to the Hebrews be thrown into the river. It is hard to imagine such wickedness, isn't it?

One day, in a certain Hebrew home, a beautiful baby boy was born.

For three months, the mother hid the baby in the house. She told her other two children, Aaron, a son, and Miriam, a daughter, that they must not breathe a word to anyone about the baby. When she could no longer hide him, she found a plan to save his life, believing that God would help her and save her beautiful little boy.

The mother sobbed, "I cannot risk letting my son be found. I shall make him a basket of reeds and set him afloat on the river. Some good person may find him."

And so the mother made a little boat of reeds, and she daubed it with pitch so that it would be watertight. She gently laid the beautiful baby in the basket.

Then the Hebrew mother kissed her son gently, and set the basket boat upon the water. As she watched it float away down the river, she prayed silently.

"Watch over my baby, God," she said. "Somehow, someway, let him grow to be a man."

She watched the little basket until it was out of sight, and then she went sadly back to her house.

The baby's sister, Miriam, watched from a distance of see what would happen to the baby. Soon after her mother had set the little basket boat afloat on the water, Miriam saw a beautiful young woman come to the river to wash herself. With her were several young women.

"It is the daughter of the great Pharaoh," thought Miriam. "Oh, dear, surely now my little baby brother will be found and killed!"

But Miriam was mistaken. For the Pharaoh's daughter was not like her father. She was as good and kind as she was beautiful. As she dipped her hands into the river, she saw something moving out on the water.

"Look," she cried to her handmaidens. "There is a little basket floating in the water." She sent one of her maids to bring it to her, so that she might see what was in the basket.

The handmaiden brought the basket to her mistress, and when the Princess looked inside, the rosy face of a beautiful baby looked up at her, crying. Pharaoh's daughter's heart was softened, and she held the child close to her.

"Oh, what a beautiful little baby you are," she crooned to it, and when the baby reached up one of its fat little hands and tugged at her lovely long hair, the Princess's eyes filled with tears. "It must be a Hebrew baby."

She was full of pity for the child.

The baby's sister Miriam had crept closer and closer, and she overheard the Princess say these words. She ran forward and cried:

"Your Highness, I know where there is a Hebrew woman who can nurse this child. Shall I call her?"

"Yes, yes, have her come at once," cried the Princess. And so little Miriam ran back to her home and told her mother about the wonderful thing that had happened. The mother was overjoyed. "God has answered my prayer," she cried.

The Princess said to the mother:

"Take the child home and nurse him and I shall pay you good wages for this service."

How glad the Hebrew mother was to take her child home! No one could harm her boy now, for he was protected by the princess of Egypt, the daughter of the king.

When the child was large enough to leave his mother, Pharaoh's daughter took him into her own home in the palace. She named him "Moses," a word that means, "Drawn out," because he was drawn out of the water.

MOSES AND JETHRO

Moses gained all the knowledge that the Egyptians had to give. In the court of the cruel king who had made slaves of the Israelites, God's people, there was growing up an Israelite boy who would someday set his people free.

Although Moses grew up among the Egyptians and gained their learning, he loved his own people, and his mother and his sister and brother. They were poor and were hated and were slaves, but he loved them: they were the people who served the Lord God, while the Egyptians worshiped idols and animals. Strange it was that so wise a people as these should bow down and pray to an ox or to a cat or to a snake, as did the Egyptians!

One day, Moses saw an Egyptian beating a Hebrew slave. "Stop!" he cried. "Can't you see that man is older and weaker than you are!"

But the Egyptian just sneered at Moses. Moses became so angry that he struck the Egyptian a blow that killed him. No one else was there, and the Hebrew helped Moses bury the body in the sand.

Not long after this, Moses saw two Hebrews fighting in the street, but when he tried to stop them, one of the men said to him:

"Who are you to tell us what to do? Mind your own business! Or maybe you would like to kill one of us as you did the Egyptian!"

Being slaves didn't do the Hebrews much good either!

The secret was out. What if the Pharaoh heard that Moses had killed an Egyptian? Moses knew the king of Egypt would order him to be killed as punishment. He knew he must hide somewhere!

So Moses fled to the land of Midian. He stopped to rest one day beside a well. As he was sitting on the ground enjoying a cool drink of water, he heard the sound of women's voices nearby. Soon Moses saw seven young women come to the well to get water. They were the seven daughters of Jethro, the priest of Midian. They had come to the well to get water for their father's sheep. But some of the shepherds who were at the well tried to drive the girls away. Moses came to their rescue and drove the shepherds away, and helped them water their

flock. The young women thanked Moses and went home to tell their father about the kind man who had helped them.

"But why did you not bring the man to this house," cried Jethro. "Go fetch him at once and we shall give him food and drink!"

And so it happened that Moses came to live in Jethro's house. Jethro was very fond of Moses, and put him in charge of all his flocks. Later, Moses married one of Jethro's daughters, Zipporah, and had a son, Gershom.

It must have been a great change in the life of Moses, after he had spent many years in a palace as a prince, to go out into the wilderness of Midian and live there as a shepherd. He saw no crowded cities, no pyramids nor temples of Egypt, nor the great river Nile. For forty years Moses wandered about the land of Midian with his flocks, often sleeping at night on the ground, and looking up by day to the great mountains.

THE BURNING BUSH

All though those years, while Moses was feeding his flock in Midian, the people of Israel were still bearing heavy burdens and working as slaves in Egypt, making bricks and building cities. The king who had begun the harsh treatment of the Israelites died, but another king took his place, and was just as cruel. He was also a Pharaoh, for this was a title, like "King," by which all the Egyptian rulers were known.

But God had not meant for Moses to stay in the hills tending sheep for long. One day, Moses was watching his sheep near Mount Horeb. Suddenly, he heard a loud crackling noise. He looked behind him, and there just a few feet away he saw a large bush on fire. The red flames crackled and leaped high into the air but the bush itself was not burnt. Moses was startled to hear a great voice coming right out of the burning bush!

"Moses, Moses!" He listened and said, "Here I am."

The voice said, "Moses, do not come nearer; take your shoes from your feet, for you are standing on holy ground."

So Moses took off his shoes and stood before the burning bush. And the voice came from the bush, saying:

"I am the God of your father, the God of Abraham, and of Isaac, and of Jacob. I have seen the wrongs and the cruelty that My people have suffered in Egypt, and I have heard their cry on account of their taskmasters. And I am coming to set them free from the land of the Egyptians, and to bring them up to their own land, the land of Canaan, a good land, and large. Come now, and I will send you to Pharaoh, the king of Egypt, and you shall lead my people out of Egypt."

Moses hid his face, and he said:

"Who am I that I should go to Pharaoh? What shall I say to him?"

And God answered:

"I will be with you. You must tell Pharaoh to let my people go."

Then Moses cried out:

"I am afraid the people will not believe me when I tell them of this wonderful burning bush! How am I to make them believe that God spoke to me and chose me for their leader?"

Moses was a modest man.

"Moses!" commanded God. "Take your rod and throw it on the ground with all your strength!"

Moses was puzzled, but he did as God told him. He threw his rod to the ground. The rod turned into a serpent! Moses turned and ran away from it.

But God called Moses and said:

"Do not be afraid! Put forth your hand and take the serpent by the tail!"

Moses fearfully obeyed. As his hand closed over the snake's tail it became a rod again in Moses' hand!

Then God said to Moses:

"Put your hand inside your shirt!"

Moses put his hand inside his shirt, and when he drew it out, it was covered with sores.

"It is leprosy!" cried Moses. He was terribly frightened, for there was no cure for this terrible disease. The people who had it were called "Unclean" by all others, and nobody would go near them.

"Fear not!" cried the Voice of God from the burning bush. "Put your hand back inside your shirt!"

Moses put his hand inside his shirt again. When he drew it out the second time, it was clean and well and the sores were gone! Moses breathed a great sigh of relief.

But Moses was still unwilling to go, because he was afraid that no one would believe him, and because he did not feel himself to be fit for such a great task. And he said to the Lord:

"O Lord, thou knowest that I am not a good speaker; I am slow of speech, and cannot talk before men."

And God said, "Am not I the Lord, who made man's

mouth? Go, and I will be with your lips, and will teach you what to say."

But Moses still hesitated, and he said, "O Lord, choose some other man for this great work; I am not able to do it."

And God said, "You have a brother, whose name is Aaron. He can speak well. Even now he is coming to see you in the wilderness. Let him help you and speak for you. Let him do the speaking, and do you show the signs which I have given you. And take this rod with you in your hand, for with it you will do many wonders!"

So Moses went to Jethro, his father-in-law, and told him about the burning bush. Old Jethro was very proud of his son-in-law, and said to him.

"Go in peace!"

Then Moses began the journey back to Egypt. Little did he dream of the dangers before him, or the hardships he would have to overcome before the Children of Israel found their Promised Land!

THE TEN TERRIBLE PLAGUES

After God spoke to Moses from the burning bush on the mountainside, Moses said good-bye to his father-in-law, Jethro, and started on his journey back to Egypt. His brother Aaron came to meet him, for God had spoken to Aaron and had told him that Moses was returning to Egypt to become the leader of the Children of Israel. The two brothers were very happy to see each other after the long years that had passed. Moses told Aaron about the many wonders God had shown him; the burning bush, and the rod turned into a serpent then back into a rod again.

When they reached Egypt, the brothers gathered together all the families of Israel, and Aaron told them that Moses had been chosen by God to lead them to their Promised Land.

But when Moses and Aaron went to Pharaoh and told him that their God had said he must let them lead the Children of Israel out of Egypt, the cruel king laughed at them and said:

"I know nothing of this God of yours. Who is He to tell the king of all Egypt what to do! I shall not let the Israelite slaves go free!"

Then Moses and Aaron went before Pharaoh again and Pharaoh said:

"Why should I believe these stories you tell me?"

"Watch, and you shall see how mighty is our God," said Moses. Then he turned to Aaron and said:

"Cast your rod to the ground!"

Pharaoh drew back in amazement for Aaron's rod had turned into a serpent. Then he became angry and called all his magicians and wise men together and ordered them to cast their rods upon the ground. When they did so, their rods also turned into serpents. But Aaron's serpent ate up all the others and then became a rod again. Pharaoh called Moses and Aaron clever magicians, and told them that they could not take his slaves, the Israelites, out of Egypt.

Then God told Moses to tell Aaron to lift up the rod and strike the waters of the river from which the people of Egypt got their drinking water. When Aaron and Moses struck the river, the people were amazed to see the water turn to blood. All the fish in the river died and the water had an evil smell. But Pharaoh still would not let the children of Israel go, because his magicians could do the same thing.

So the Lord spoke to Moses again:

"Tell your brother Aaron to smite the waters of the land and bring many frogs up into the people's houses and these frogs will go into the houses and beds, the food and the ovens and will plague everyone in Egypt."

And Aaron stretched out his hand over the waters and the frogs came up and covered all the land.

Imagine what it would be like to have thousands and thousands of slimy frogs hopping and crawling all over everything, and jumping on your face at night while you slept. The Pharaoh could not bear this terrible plague of frogs any longer and, because his magicians couldn't do away with them, He called Moses and Aaron to him and said:

"Tell your God to take away the frogs and I will let the children of Israel go."

Moses was filled with joy. At last, after all the terrible struggle, he would lead his people out of slavery. He asked God to send the frogs back into the rivers and streams. But when he saw that the frogs were gone, the Pharaoh did not keep his promise.

Then God became angry and said to Moses:

"Tell Aaron to stretch out his rod and smite the dust of the land and it shall turn into gnats."

Aaron did as Moses told him and all the dust of Egypt

turned into gnats. These horrible little insects were everywhere. In people's hair, on their bodies, on all the animals. Yes, even on the great Pharaoh, who did not look so high and mighty as he jumped up and down, scratching first his head, then his feet, then his face. The gnats flew all over and bit the animals and all the people so that they itched and cried out for help. Pharaoh commanded his magicians to rid the country of the gnats but they could not. They were so busy scratching that they couldn't try very hard anyway!

Then the magicians said to Pharaoh:

"Surely this is the work of the God of the Israelites."

But even then Pharaoh would not let the children of Israel go.

Then God sent a plague of flies and wild creatures. Again Pharaoh begged Moses to tell his God to make the plague go away.

But even after God had answered Moses' prayer and taken away the plague, the Pharaoh broke his promise again, and said he would keep his slaves in Egypt.

Then God made all the cattle of the Egyptians die, but saved the cattle that belonged to the Israelites. Still

the Pharaoh hardened his heart against Moses and his people.

Next, God sent a plague of boils. Even Pharaoh's magicians had these painful boils on their hands and faces and bodies. But Pharaoh was very stubborn, and shook his head, "No," when Moses asked him to let his people go.

Then God told Moses to tell the Pharaoh that there would be a great hailstorm that would kill all the cattle and animals left out in the fields. When the people heard this, those who believed Moses took their animals in, but those who laughed at him left their animals in the fields. And Moses stretched forth his rod toward Heaven, and God sent thunder, and hail, and lightning that ran along the ground in great tongues of flame. Only in the land of Goshen where the children of Israel kept their herds and flocks was there no hail. It is hard to imagine a man as wicked as the Pharaoh. Even after the great hail he would not free the Hebrew slaves.

Then God sent a great plague of locusts that ate up every green thing in the land of Egypt. This really alarmed the Pharaoh, and he called Moses to him and said:

"I am sorry that I kept breaking my promises. Please ask your God to forgive me this once, and I will let the Hebrews go."

God sent a strong west wind, which swept away all the locusts, and drove them into the Red Sea.

But as soon as the locusts were gone, Pharaoh laughed at Moses and Aaron and drove them from his palace. Then God told Moses to stretch forth his hand toward Heaven, and lo and behold, a thick darkness came over all the land.

While all these terrible plagues were falling upon the people of Egypt, the Israelites in the land of Goshen were living in safety under God's care. The waters there were not made into blood; nor did the flies and the locusts trouble them. While all was dark in the rest of Egypt, in the land of Goshen the sun was shining.

The Egyptians knew that the Lord God of the Israelites was watching over his own people.

After three whole days of darkness Pharaoh called Moses to him again and said:

"You may take your people and go. But leave your flocks and herds here in Egypt." But when Moses said they would need their cows and sheep and could not leave them, Pharaoh once more hardened his heart and told Moses never to show his face to him again or he would have him killed.

Moses said, "Good, I will never see you again!"

Moses left the Pharaoh's palace in despair. But God spoke to him once more and said:

"Fear not, for I shall now send a plague more terrible than any other upon the Egyptians. About midnight, I will go into the midst of Egypt, and all the firstborn in the land shall die, from the firstborn of Pharaoh down to the firstborn of the servants and even the firstborn of the animals. But among the children of Israel, none shall die. And the people of Egypt will rise up in grief and demand that Pharaoh let you take the children of Israel out of their land."

Moses was very sad that such a terrible thing must be done to soften Pharaoh's stubborn heart, and on that terrible night that the firstborn were slain, there was not a house in all Egypt that did not have someone dead in it. But there were no dead among the children of Israel. At last, the Pharaoh knew that this God of Israel was far more powerful than he, and he was afraid. The cruel king called for Moses and Aaron in the middle of the night crying, for his oldest child had died.

"Go!" he cried. "Go out of Egypt with your people and take your flocks and herds and everything that you need!"

THE EXODUS

Suddenly, early in the morning, the Israelites went out of the land after four hundred and thirty years in Egypt. They went out in order, like a great army, family by family and tribe by tribe, after joyfully gathering everything they owned, even the bread which had been started that evening, but which didn't have time to rise. Because the children of Israel took the flat, unleavened bread with them out of Egypt, unleavened bread is still eaten at Passover time, in memory of that far-off day when Moses led his people out of slavery.

And the Lord God went before the host of Israel to guide them, as they marched out of Egypt. In the daytime they were guided by a great cloud, like a pillar, in front, and at night by a pillar of fire. So both by day and night, as they saw the cloudy and fiery pillar going before them, they could say, "Our Lord, the God of heaven and earth, goes before us."

When the pillar of cloud stopped, they knew it was a sign that they were to pause in their journey and rest. So they set up their tents and waited until the cloud should rise up and go forward. When they looked and saw that the pillar of cloud was higher up in the air, and as though moving forward, they took down their tents and formed in order for the march. Thus the pillar was like a guide by day and a guard by night.

You remember that when Joseph died he commanded the Israelites not to bury his body in Egypt, but to keep it unburied, as long as they should stay in the land. When they were going out of Egypt, Moses ordered the people to take with them the coffin which held the embalmed body of Joseph.

After the Children of Israel had left Egypt, Pharaoh missed his slaves, saying:

"What have we done, to let our slaves go?"

He was afraid, too, that such a large number of people might join up with his enemies. So Pharaoh ordered his

army to prepare, and chased the Israelites. The Israelites were encamped to prepare to rest beside the Red Sea, when they saw a great cloud of dust on the horizon. Then someone shouted:

"We are lost! It is the Pharaoh's army come to take us back to slavery!"

A great cry of anguish went up from these weary people who had waited so long for their freedom, only, they feared, to lose it after so short a time.

"Fear not," declared Moses. "Stand still and see how God will save you. As for the Egyptians, whom you now see following you, you will never see them again. The Lord will fight for you, and you shall stand still and see your enemies slain."

That night the pillar of fire, which was before the host of Israel, went behind them and stood between the camp of the Egyptians and the camp of the Israelites. To the children of Israel it was bright and dazzling with the glory of the Lord, but to the Egyptians the pillar was dark and terrible; and they dared not enter it.

And all that night there blew over the sea a mighty east wind so that the water was blown away; and when the morning came, there was a ridge of dry land between water on one side and water on the other, making a road across the sea to the land beyond, and on each side of the road the water stood like walls, as if to keep their enemies away from them.

Then Moses told the people to go forward. They walked across the Red Sea as on dry land and passed safely over into the wilderness on the other side. So God brought his people out of Egypt into a land that they had never seen.

When the Egyptians saw them marching into the sea, they followed with their chariots and their horses. But the sand was no longer hard; it had become soft, and their chariot wheels were caught in it, and many wheels broke off the chariots. And the horses sank in the mire and fell down, so that the army was in confusion; and all were frightened. The soldiers cried out:

"Let us fly from the face of the Israelites! The Lord is fighting for them and against us!"

By this time, all the Israelites had passed through the Red Sea and were standing on the high ground beyond it, looking at their enemies slowly struggling through the sand, all in one heaped-up mass of men and horses and chariots. Then Moses lifted up his hand, and at once a great tide of water swept up from the sea on the south; the road over which the Israelites had walked in safety was covered with water; and the host of Pharaoh, with all his chariots and his horses and their riders, were drowned in the sea, before the eyes of the people of Israel. They saw the dead bodies of the Egyptians tossed up by the waves on the shore.

Moses wrote a fine song, and all the people sang it together over their great victory, which God had wrought for them. Miriam, Moses' sister, and all the women sang and danced:

I will sing unto the Lord, for He hath triumphed gloriously
The horse and his rider hath He thrown into the sea,
The Lord is my strength and might,
And He is become my salvation.

THE WATERS OF BITTERNESS

How happy the Children of Israel were, as they marched along, getting farther and farther away from Egypt each day! They sang songs of praise to God. They shouted and laughed and said to each other:

"We have the greatest man who ever lived for our leader. Moses was truly chosen by God to lead us to our Promised Land!"

So Moses led the Israelites from the Red Sea into the wilderness of Shur; and they went three days in the wilderness and found no water.

Such a host of men and women and children, with their flocks, would need much water, and they found very little.

They saw some springs of water in the distance and ran to drink of it, for they were very thirsty. But when they tasted, they found it bitter, so that they could not drink it. Then the people cried to Moses:

"What are we to drink? Have you brought us into the desert to die of thirst?"

And Moses cried to the Lord; and the Lord showed Moses a tree, and told him to cut it down and throw it into the water. Moses did so, and then the water became fresh and pure and good, so that the people could drink it. This place they named Marah, a word which means "Bitterness," because of the water which they found there.

After passing Marah, they came to another and more pleasant place. There they saw twelve springs of fresh water and a grove of seventy palm trees around them. And there they rested under the cool shade of the palm trees.

MANNA FROM HEAVEN

For nearly two months the Israelites journeyed on. The springs and oases were soon left behind, and the wanderers came to the great wilderness of Sin, which lies between Elim and Sinai. This land was dry and dusty. The days were hot and there was not a drop of water nor a bite of food to be found anywhere. The women and children wept, and the men began to grumble and complain among themselves.

Then the people cried out against Moses and his brother Aaron and said:

"Why have you led us into this terrible wilderness, where we shall surely die of thirst and starvation? We would have been better off if we had stayed in Egypt. At least we had plenty to eat there, and lots of good clear water!"

Then the Lord spoke to Moses, saying, "I have heard the murmuring of the children of Israel. Speak to them and say: 'At evening you will eat meat, and in the morning you will have your fill of bread, and so you will know that I am the Lord your God.' "

That evening, the Israelites noticed a gray cloud far off in the sky. The cloud came closer and closer. Then the men began shouting to each other in great excitement:

"Look! Look! It is not a cloud at all! It is a great flock of quail. It is the meat God promised us."

That evening, many flocks of quail flew over the place where the Children of Israel were camping, and the men caught enough of the birds so that everyone had meat to eat.

And so the Children of Israel received the meat God had promised to send them.

The next morning when the people looked out of their tents, they saw all around the camp, on the sand, little white flakes, like snow or frost. They had never seen anything like it before and they said, just as anybody would say, "What is it?" In the language of the Israelites, the Hebrew language, "What is it?" is the word "manhu." So the people said to one another "Man hu? Man hu?" And this gave a name afterward to what they saw, the name *Manna*.

And Moses said to them, "This is the bread which the Lord has given you to eat. Go out and gather it, as much as you need. But take only as much as you need for today, for it will not keep, and God will give you more tomorrow."

So the people went out and gathered the manna. They cooked it in various ways, baking it and boiling it; and the taste of it was like wafers flavored with honey. Some took more than they needed, not trusting God's word that there would be more on the next day. But that which was left over after it was gathered, spoiled and smelled bad, so that it was useless. This was to teach the people that each day they should trust God for their daily bread.

But the manna which was left on the ground did not spoil. When the sun came up, it melted away, just as frost or snowflakes. Before the sixth day of the week came, Moses said to all the people.

"Tomorrow, on the sixth day of the week, take twice as much manna as usual; for the next day is the Lord's Sabbath, the day of rest, and the manna will not come on that day."

So the next morning, all the people went out as before to gather the manna. On that day, they found that the manna which was not used did not spoil, but kept fresh until the next morning.

From then on the manna was on the ground every morning, and the Children of Israel gathered it each day. Each man gathered just enough for his family to eat in one day. On the sixth day, there was twice as much manna, just as God had promised. Some of the people disobeyed Moses and went out into the wilderness on the morning of the Sabbath day, but there was no manna to be found that morning. God spoke to Moses once more.

"Tell the people they must rest on the Sabbath day. They must not go out to gather food."

During the forty years that the Children of Israel wandered in the wilderness, they ate manna, which God always sent them. The manna looked like small white seeds and tasted just like wafers made with honey.

Once more, God had proved to Moses and his people

that if they prayed for help, they would receive it. Moses did not forget to thank God for the quail and the manna, and he said to his brother Aaron:

"Take a pot and put manna into it, and lay it before the Lord, so that all the people who live after us can see how God fed His children in the wilderness."

THE TEN GREAT LAWS

As they wandered on and on, there were many times when Moses thought he would have to give up. Sometimes fierce desert tribes attacked their camp during the night. But the men of Israel always drove these wild desert warriors away.

One day, three months after they had left Egypt, the Children of Israel came to the wilderness of Sinai. They made camp at the foot of a great mountain. That evening, Moses went up the mountain, and God spoke to him. God said to Moses:

"Moses, listen carefully to what I tell you," cried God. "Go among the people and give them My blessing. Tell them: 'You have seen what I did to the Egyptians, and how I brought you out of slavery. If you do what I command, you shall be a holy nation.' Tell them to purify themselves and to be ready. On the third day, I shall come down, so that everyone will see, on the mountain of Sinai. But nobody must come up into the mountain. The one who comes into the mountain shall die. When I call you, Moses, you must come, for what I shall tell you is of great importance."

On the morning of the third day, all the people of Israel gathered on the mountainside.

Suddenly, a great crash of thunder sounded. Lightning flashed and the ground trembled so hard beneath the people's feet that they fell to their knees and hid their faces in their arms. A great red flame rose from the mountain top and clouds of thick, black smoke rolled up toward the sky. Then Moses heard the voice of the Lord:

"Moses! Come to the mountaintop."

Up and up the mountain Moses climbed, and finally the people could no longer see him. Moses had disappeared into the thick black clouds and the red flames. When Moses reached the mountaintop, he was trembling, for the black smoke and flames were all around him. He bowed his head and God spoke these words to him:

"Moses, I shall tell you of ten great commandments. These are My laws and you must tell your people of them, and the children and their children's children must teach these ten great laws to all the nations of the earth. Listen to My commandments!"

Then God gave Moses two stone tablets, with the ten great laws carved on them. Forty days and forty nights Moses had been with God on the mountaintop. He took the stone tablets and started his journey back down the mountain to the Children of Israel.

Thousands of years have passed since God gave Moses the Ten Commandments, and all the nations of the world know these laws. No better laws have ever been written, for the Ten Commandments are God's own laws. If everyone always remembered these laws and obeyed them, what a wonderful world this would be!

THE TEN COMMANDMENTS

1. *Thou shalt* have no other gods before Me.
2. *Thou shalt* not make graven images, or bow down to them.
3. *Thou shalt* not take the name of God vain.
4. Remember the Sabbath day to keep it holy. In it *thou* shalt do no work.
5. Honor *thy* father and *thy* mother.
6. *Thou shalt* not kill.
7. *Thou shalt* not commit adultery.
8. *Thou shalt* not steal.
9. *Thou shalt* not bear false witness against *thy* neighbor.
10. *Thou shalt* not covet anything which belongs to another person.

THE GOLDEN CALF

The Children of Israel were very anxious for Moses to return to them from the top of Mount Sinai, where he had gone to talk with God. But when many days passed and their leader did not come back, the people grew restless, and they grumbled among themsleves.

"What has happened to Moses?" they asked.

"Yes," one complained, "why does he stay so long? Perhaps he has deserted his people!"

"We have nobody to lead us now," cried still another.

Bad talk aways spreads fast, just like fire in dry grass, and soon the whole camp was buzzing with complaints about Moses and his long stay on the mountaintop.

Finally, some of the people went to Aaron, Moses' brother, and said:

"Moses has not returned. Perhaps he never will. We need a god to worship. We want someone to lead us! Give us a god who will tell us what to do!"

You see, while the Children of Israel had lived in Egypt, they had seen the Egyptians worshiping statues of animals and all sorts of idols made of stone and metal. They felt lost without something to kneel to, and their faith was not yet strong enough to trust in their one true God. They wanted something they could see!

Aaron saw that the people were restless and ready to start trouble. He knew he must think of some way to keep them quiet until Moses returned.

"Very well," said Aaron, "I will make you a god if you must have something to worship. Bring me your gold jewelry and your gold rings."

Aaron did not think the people would give up their gold, but they did. Then Aaron built a hot fire and put all the gold rings and jewelry into it. The people watched as their gold melted and became a mass of hot metal. Then Aaron shaped this liquid gold into a calf. He set the Golden Calf upon its feet and said:

"There is the god you asked for! Now let him lead you out of the wilderness!"

The people cried aloud with joy, for they foolishly believed this metal animal that had no life at all, nor a mind nor a soul, was their god!

They shouted and sang and danced around the golden calf and threw themselves on the ground and worshiped it. The sight made Aaron turn his head away in disgust. He sighed deeply.

"How soon they have forgotten," he said to himself, "how Moses led them so bravely, how he got food from heaven for them. My poor brother's heart will be broken when he sees how wicked his beloved people have become!"

But God had already seen the people's wickedness, and He said to Moses in anger:

"Get back to your people! They are worshiping an idol instead of Me. I shall destroy them all, for they are wicked and worthless! They have forgotten all I have done for them!"

"Oh, no, please do not destroy my people," begged Moses. "Remember your promise to Abraham and Isaac, to lead the Children of Israel to the Promised Land. The people are good. It is just that they are weary now of wandering. I will go down to them and they will see the ten great laws and rejoice and praise Your holy Name again!"

God promised to forgive the Children of Israel and not destroy them, but He was still very angry.

Moses hurried back down the mountain, with the stone tablets in his hand. As he came near the Israelites' camp, he heard loud singing and shouting, and he saw people dancing wildly around something that glistened brightly in the sunlight. Moses pushed through the crowd, and saw the golden calf. He was so angry that he raised the great stone tablets high above his head and flung them to the ground. They broke into a thousand pieces! Then Moses took the golden calf and threw it into the fire. The people watched their foolish idol as it melted.

Moses ground the melted gold into powder. He sprinkled the bitter powder on the drinking water and

commanded the Children of Israel to drink! Then Moses
turned to Aaron:

"What led you to such an act as this?" said Moses.
"Why did you let the people persuade you to make them
an image for worship?"

And Aaron said, "Do not be angry with me; you know
how the hearts of this people are set to do evil. They
came to me and said, 'Make us a god,' and I said to them,
'Give me whatever gold you have.' So they gave it to
me, and I threw the gold into the fire, and this calf came
out!"

Then Moses stood at the entrance to the camp and
called out:

"Whoever is on the Lord's side, let him come and
stand by me!" Then one whole tribe out of the twelve
tribes of Israel, the tribe of Levi, all sprung from Levi,
one of Jacob's sons, came and stood beside Moses. And
Moses said to them:

"Draw your swords and go through the camp and kill
everyone whom you find bowing down to the idol. Spare
no one. Slay your friends and your neighbors, if they are
worshiping the image."

And on that day three thousand of the worshipers of
the idol were slain by the sons of Levi.

Then Moses said to the people, "You have sinned a
great sin; but I will go to the Lord and I will ask him
to forgive your sin."

Then Moses prayed to God and asked him to forgive
the Children of Israel. But God would not completely
forgive the people, and He told Moses that from now on,
He would not lead them, but would have one of His
angels do it instead. When Moses told the people what
God had said, they were very sad. They knew they had
brought about their own punishment by being so foolish
and wicked. They took all their jewels and offered them
to Moses to prove to him how sorry they were for doing
wrong.

God finally did forgive the Children of Israel, as He always forgives anyone who is truly sorry for breaking His laws. God told Moses to come back to the mountain top and He would give him two more stone tablets to replace the broken ones.

So Moses went up a second time into the holy mount; and there God talked with him again. Moses stayed forty days on this second meeting with God, as he had stayed in the mountain forty days before. And all this time, while God was talking with Moses, the people waited in the camp; and they did not again set up any idol for worship.

Once more Moses came down the mountain, bringing the two stone tablets upon which God has written the words of his law, the Ten Commandments. And Moses had been so close to God's glory and had been so long in the blaze of God's light, that when he came into the camp of Israel, his face was shining, though he did not know it. The people could not look on Moses face, it was so dazzling. And Moses found that when he talked with the people it was needful for him to wear a veil over his face. When Moses went to talk with God, he took off the veil; but while he spoke with the people, he kept his face covered, for it shone as the sun.

THE HOLY ARK

After Moses brought down the tablets of stone from Mount Sinai, with the laws of God carved upon them, the children of Israel said to one another:

"Now we have God's own laws to guide us and tell us what is right and what is wrong. But something might happen to our precious tablets. We might lose them, or leave them behind when we move from one place to another. How shall we keep them safe?"

God said to Moses:

"Have the people build a Holy Tent, or Tabernacle, so that it may be carried with you as you journey to the Promised Land. Build this Tabernacle very carefully Let everyone help, every man and woman and even the small children. Decorate the Tabernacle with gold and fine linen. When it is finished, find the sweetest and most beautiful wood, and of this wood build an Ark. Place the sacred tablets within the Ark. Then put the Ark in the center of the Tabernacle and before it hang a veil. This shall be your Holy of Holies."

When Moses told the Children of Israel what God had said, there was great rejoicing. Every man and woman began at once to do his or her part to help build the Holy of Holies. The men engraved shining gold, the women wove fine linens, and the children held the skeins of flax or carried things back and forth to help.

When the tent was finished, it was covered with curtains and goats' hair and rams' skins which had been dyed red. Inside the tent the people hung ten curtains of blue and purple and bright scarlet. Then the veil was hung in the very center of the tent. Now it was time to build the Holy Ark.

God decided upon the acacia tree, because this tree was very beautiful and because the wood from it has a sweet smell. The Ark was built with great care by the finest carpenters. Bezalel, one of the children of Israel who was a great artist, taught the people how to make everything just as beautiful as possible.

At last, the Ark was finished. Very carefully, Aaron, the brother of Moses, and the High Priest of the Israelites, lifted the Holy Ark and carried it into the Tabernacle, where he set it gently down behind the silken veil. Then an altar was built of wood, and covered with gold and brass; brass dishes were placed upon this altar, for the sacrifices of food.

The Children of Israel all gathered in front of the Tabernacle to look at the beautiful work they had done. They were very proud, and well they might be! The gold glistened in the sun. The beautiful red and gold and purple colors of the curtains were like a glorious rainbow.

There was not a man, woman, or child who had not worked hard to make the Holy of Holies a beautiful and perfect place.

Moses held up his hand, and everyone was very still. Then Aaron, the High Priest, came forward, carrying the sacred tablets. He wore the dazzling breast plate, the ephod, the Children of Israel had made for him, with twelve sparkling jewels set into it, each jewel bearing the name of a different tribe of Israel. Aaron stepped inside the Holy of Holies, and Moses spoke to the people:

"Surely God must be pleased with His children on this day," he said, "for our work is done and our Holy of Holies is beautiful indeed; now the Hebrews are united into one people. Our sacred laws which God has given us are safe inside our Tabernacle, where they must remain forever and ever. Nobody must ever enter the Holy of Holies except Aaron, the High Priest. Once a year, on the Day of Atonement, Aaron will go into the Tabernacle and make the sacred offerings as God has commanded."

Then the Children of Israel gave thanks to God, and the Levites played holy music and sang hymns of praise. Aaron, the High Priest, brought the sacred tablets inside the Holy of Holies.

Inside the Holy of Holies was a chest, made of wood and covered with plates of gold on both the outside and the inside; and with a cover of solid gold, on which stood two figures called cherubim, also made of gold. This chest was called the Ark of the Covenant, and in it Aaron placed for safekeeping the two stone tablets on which God wrote the Ten Commandments. Then Aaron came out of the Tabernacle and blessed the people; and lo and behold, a cloud came down and covered the Holy of Holies, and the Glory of God shone forth so brightly that even Moses was blinded and hid his face. Then the people knew that God was pleased, and had sent His special blessing to them. When the cloud lifted, several of the strongest men lifted the Holy Tent upon their shoulders, and the Children of Israel moved on once more in search of their Promised Land.

But now they had the sacred laws of God to guide them, and they had new courage and strength. The Holy of Holies was carried with them everywhere, and the lamp inside it was kept burning always.

THE SPIES IN CANAAN

The Israelites stayed in their camp before Mount Sinai almost a year, while they were building the Tabernacle and learning God's laws given through Moses. At last the cloud over the Tabernacle rose, and the people knew that this was the sign for them to move. They took down the Tabernacle and their own tents and journeyed northward toward the land of Canaan for many days, led by the pillar of cloud by day and the pillar of fire by night.

At last they came to a place just on the border between the desert and Canaan in the wilderness of Paran called Kadesh, or Kadesh-barnea. Here they stopped to rest, for there were many springs of water and some grass for their cattle. It was an oasis in the desert. While they were waiting at Kadesh-barnea, God told Moses to send some men ahead to travel through the land as spies, and then come back and tell what they had found: what kind of land it was, what fruits and crops grew in it, and what people were living in it. The Israelites could more easily win the land if these men, after finding out about it, could act as their guides and point out the best places in it and the best plans for making war upon it. There was need of wise and bold men for such work as this, for it was full of danger.

Twelve men were chosen, one man for each tribe. One of these men was Joshua, a brave soldier of Israel and a very close friend of Moses. Another was Caleb, a man of great courage and faith in God.

The people thought they could never wait until the twelve spies came back from Canaan. Forty long days passed. And then one morning:

"Look! Look!" cried the Children of Israel. "Here come our men back from the land of Canaan! But what is that they are carrying on their shoulders?"

All the people ran to meet the twelve spies, and they gazed in wonder and delight at what two of the men carried. It was a bunch of grapes, so large that it took two men to carry it on long poles stretched between their shoulders. The grapes themselves were huge, and they shone like purple gems in the sun.

The people cried out with joy. Then their questions came pouring forth:

"Is there lots of grass?"

"Are there plums and pomegranates and other fruit?"

"Is there plenty of water?"

"Are the people tall or short?"

Moses smiled and held up his hand.

"One at a time," he said. "First of all, what of the people of this new land? Are they friendly?"

Ten of the spies looked very serious, and they shook their heads.

"No," they answered, "they are not friendly at all. They are very fierce and warlike. Their cities have great high walls around them."

But Caleb said quickly:

"What do these things matter to the brave Children of Israel, who have already fought the wilderness! Besides, we have God on our side. We must go and fight these fierce people and claim our rightful homeland."

"But Caleb!" cried the ten spies. "You saw the people yourself! They are like giants compared to us. They would trample us like ants beneath their feet!"

The people looked alarmed. Many of them were so frightened that they even talked of turning around and going back the way they had come.

Then Joshua commanded the people to be quiet.

"Have you forgotten how powerful God is?" he cried. "He has never broken a promise to us. He has been with us all the way from Egypt, just as He will be with us in the battle against the Canaanites! Why should we be afraid, with God on our side!"

But the Children of Israel would not listen. They let their fear overcome their faith in God.

WANDERERS IN THE DESERT

After the spies had brought back their report, the people were filled with fear. They cried out against Moses, and blamed him for bringing them out of the land of Egypt. They forgot all their troubles in Egypt, their toil and their slavery, and they resolved to go back to that land. They said, "Let us choose a ruler in place of Moses, who has brought us into all these evils, and let us turn back to the land of Egypt!"

Now God heard all this talk, and He became very angry. He spoke to Moses once more:

"Your people are not worthy of this beautiful land to which I have led them. I have provided them with food and water in the wilderness. I have given them wise laws to live by. They lived too long as slaves to be brave enough to trust in Me. They shall not see the Promised Land!"

But Moses still loved the people he had led for so long, and he begged God to forgive them once more.

And God said:

"How long will this people disobey and despise me? They shall not go into the good land that I have promised them. Not one of them shall enter in except Caleb and Joshua, who have been faithful to me. All of the people

who are twenty years old and over shall die in the
desert; but their little children shall grow up in the
wilderness, and when they become men, they shall enter
in and own the land that I promised to their fathers. Your
people are not worthy of the land that I have been keeping for them. Joshua shall lead your children into the
land of Canaan. And because Caleb showed another
spirit, and was true to me, and followed my will fully,
Caleb shall live to go into the land, and shall have his
choice of a home there. Tomorrow, turn back into the
desert by the way of the Red Sea."

When Moses told the Children of Israel about God's
punishment, they changed their minds in a hurry!

"No! No!" they cried. "We cannot bear another forty
years of wandering. It is too much! We will go to fight
the people of the land of Canaan right now!"

But Moses said:

"It is too late. You should have been willing to do that
in the beginning. Now God has forbidden us to go into
Canaan."

But the people would not listen. The men marched forward to Canaan. But God was not with them, and they
lost the battle. The fierce Canaanites drove them back
into the desert, and many of the Children of Israel were
killed.

Discouraged and beaten, they obeyed the Lord and Moses, and went once more into the desert.

And in the desert of Paran, on the south of the land of Canaan, the children of Israel stayed nearly forty years, because they had not trusted in the Lord.

It was not strange that the Israelites should act like children eager to go back one day and then eager to go forward the next day. Through four hundred years their spirit had been weakened by living in the land of Egypt. Their hard lot as slaves had made them unfit to care for themselves. Moses saw that they needed the free life of the wilderness to make them appreciate freedom, and that their children, growing up as free men and trained for war, would be far better fitted to win the land of promise than their fathers had shown themselves to be. So they went back into the wilderness to wait and to be trained for the work of winning their land through war.

REBELLION

Even though Moses was a great and good leader, some of the Israelites were not satisfied with the way he was doing things. Perhaps some of these people were jealous of Moses; many people are jealous of those who are great and good. Instead of trying to be good themselves, these people spend most of their time trying to make trouble, and complaining.

There were three men, Korah and Dathan and Abiram, who went to Moses with two hundred and fifty others.

"Why do you set yourself up above us? You are no better than we are," these rebels said to their leader.

Moses was very sad when he heard these words.

"Korah, and all the men with you, take censers and put incense and fire in them and go before the Tabernacle. Pray to God to show you who is holy and who is the rightful leader."

Then Moses called Dathan and Abiram also, but they would not pay any attention to him.

The next day, Korah gathered his men before the Tabernacle. The air was sweet and heavy with the smell of the burning incense. The children of Israel gathered in a great crowd to watch. Then God spoke to Moses and Aaron:

"Separate yourself from the people, for I shall destroy them."

But Moses and Aaron fell down upon their faces and cried:

"Please do not punish all the people just because a few of them are rebels against the Lord!"

Then God said:

"Tell the people to stay far away from the tents of Korah, Dathan, and Abiram."

Moses told the people to go into the hills, and away from the tents of these three men. Suddenly, a noise like thunder came, and the earth itself split open. Into the great hole in the earth fell Korah, Dathan, and Abiram, and their families. Then a terrible fire came out of the sky and destroyed every one of the two hundred and fifty rebels.

Moses was very sad, for he loved all his people. But he knew God's commands must be obeyed. He told the Children of Israel to get ready to move on in their search for the Promised Land.

THE WATER OF STRIFE

After the Children of Israel had received their sacred laws, they wandered on through the wilderness in search of their Promised Land. Finally they came to the desert of Zin. This land was hot and dry. There was no water for the people to drink. The Israelites began to complain and grumble. But Moses told them they must be patient and trust in God.

"We have been in the wilderness before without water and food," said Moses. "God has always helped us and kept us from dying of thirst or hunger."

But the people did not always have as much faith as Moses had. They became even more discontented, and began crying in loud voices to Moses and his brother Aaron:

"Would that we had died long ago! Why did you bring us to this barren land so that we must listen to our children crying for water!"

It made Moses very sad to think that the Children of Israel had forgotten so soon how long he had been their faithful leader, and how many times he had prayed to God to spare the people, even when God wanted to destroy them for their wickedness.

The people's complaints became louder and louder. Moses could bear it no longer.

"Come," he said to Aaron, "let us go to the Tabernacle and pray."

Aaron and Moses went inside the door to the Tabernacle, fell upon their faces and prayed. Then the glory of God shone all around them, and the voice of God spoke these words:

"Moses, gather the people together before a great rock. Speak to the rock, and it shall give forth water enough for the people to drink and their flocks and beasts also."

And so Moses and Aaron called the Children of Israel together before the rock. The people came, but many of them were sulky and scowling. Some of the men cast harsh glances at Moses and Aaron and whispered to each other:

"Who are these two that they set themselves up above us! Why do they not give us water!"

And others said:

"We should rebel against these leaders. It is water we want, not fancy talk!"

Now Moses heard many of these things. As he looked out over the people and thought about how long he had led them and loved them, and how much he had suffered for them and how little faith they had in him now, he was suddenly filled with a great anger against them. He lifted his rod high in the air and shook it in the faces of the people.

"Hear now, you rebels," Moses cried, "must we fetch you water from this rock?"

Then Moses struck the rock hard . . . once, twice . . . and behold! . . . the clear, cold water gushed forth and the people ran to the rock and drank their fill, and led their donkeys and sheep to drink also.

But God was displeased with Moses and spoke to him in a stern voice:

"Moses," cried God, "do you now set yourself up above Me? It was not you, but I who brought the water out of the rock. Yet you did not speak to the rock as I commanded you to, but struck it in anger, as though it were you alone who could perform miracles! Because you did not listen to my command, you will not lead the people into their Promised Land, but only to the banks of the River Jordan. Joshua will lead the Children of Israel into the land I have promised them."

These words made Moses sad indeed. He bowed his head for a long time. Then went back to the people, and the Children of Israel, with Moses leading them, continued on in their search. The place where Moses struck the rock was called Meribah, which means "strife."

Moses knew he had done wrong by calling the Children of Israel rebels, for they had been through many trials and hardships. They had loved their leader and followed him throughout the long years in the wilderness. Moses did not complain about God's punishment. He knew that he deserved it, and he made up his mind to try to understand his people better and never to be angry with them again. Moses also knew that the true leader of the Israelites was not he, but God. God put the words of wisdom into his mouth; God put the power into Moses' rod so that when it struck a rock, water spurted forth, and when it was raised over an ocean, the waters parted. If it had not been for God's help, Moses would have been a shepherd all his life, tending his father-in-law's sheep, and the Children of Israel would still have been slaves in Egypt.

About this time, Miriam, the sister of Moses and Aaron, died at Kadesh-barnea. You remember that when she was a little girl, she helped to save the baby Moses, her brother, from the river. She also led the women in singing the Song of Moses after the crossing of the Red Sea. And soon after her death, Moses and Aaron, and Eleazar,

Aaron's son, walked together up a mountain called Hor; and on the top of the mountain Moses took the priestly robes off Aaron, and placed them on his son Eleazar; and there on the top of Mount Hor, Aaron died, and Moses and Eleazar buried him. Then they came down to the camp and Eleazar took his father's place as the priest.

THE STORY OF BALAAM

The years passed swiftly, and the small children of the Hebrews who had left Egypt with Moses so long ago had now grown to be fine strong men and women. The children of Israel had fought and won many battles, with God always on their side. The peoples of other lands began to fear these Israelites and their wise leader.

As the wanderers neared the Land of Canaan, they came to the country of Moab. This people had sprung from Lot, the nephew of Abraham, of whom we read in earlier stories. In the five hundred years since Lot's time, his family or descendants had become a people who were called Moabites, just as Jacob's descendants were the Israelites. The Moabites were filled with alarm and fear as they saw this mighty host of Israel marching around their land, conquering the country and encamping on their border. The Moabites were ruled by a king whose name was Balak, and he tried to form some plan for driving away the people of Israel from that region.

When Balak heard the Israelites were camped near the borders of his country, he said to himself:

"These people seem to cover the earth! But I shall not allow them to come into my kingdom! I must send messengers to the wise prophet and have him come here to curse these Israelites!"

Now the name of this famous prophet, who lived many miles away from Moab, was Balaam. This man was known far and wide as a prophet, that is, a man who talked with God, and heard God's voice, and spoke from God, as did Moses. People believed that whatever Balaam said was sure to come to pass; but they did not know that Balaam could only speak what God gave him to speak.

Balaam was very wise, and he also feared God, and did not want to do anything against God's wishes. So when King Balak's messengers arrived at Balaam's house and told the great prophet about the Children of Israel, Balaam said:

"I cannot tell you right now whether I will go with you to King Balak or not. You must remain here at my house overnight. I shall wait for God to tell me what to do."

Balak's messengers agreed to stay. But that night, as Balaam lay on his bed, thinking about King Balak and the Children of Israel, he heard God's voice say:

"Do not go with these men! Do not curse the people of Israel, for they are blessed!"

The next morning, Balaam said to the messengers:

"I am sorry I cannot go with you. God has told me not to curse the Children of Israel!"

But when the messengers returned home and told King Balak what Balaam had said, the king was very troubled.

"I will send princes with much silver to Balaam," he cried. "He must come to me and curse the Israelites!"

When the princes arrived at Balaam's house, bearing fine gifts and silver, Balaam said to them:

"Even if King Balak gave me his whole house full of silver and gold, I still must do what God tells me to do. You must stay at my house overnight and I will listen for God's voice."

That night, God said to Balaam:

"If the men ask you to go with them, rise up and go. But listen for the words I will tell you to say!"

And so the next morning, Balaam saddled his donkey and set out with the princes on the journey to Moab. But all of a sudden, Balaam's donkey began to act very strangely. First she turned off the road and wandered into a field. Balaam scolded her and made her get back on the road. Shortly after this, as they were facing down a narrow road, with a wall on either side, the donkey stopped still in the road, and then turned and walked right into the wall, crushing Balaam's foot against the stones.

"You stupid donkey!" cried Balaam in great anger. But the donkey was not as stupid as Balaam thought. For she had seen something in the road that Balaam could not see. Twice, the donkey had seen a mighty angel, with a great shining sword, standing right in her path. A third time the donkey saw the angel, and this time, the road was so narrow, there was no place for her to go, and she fell down under Balaam. Then Balaam was indeed angry. He hit the poor donkey with a stick. But God put words into the donkey's mouth, and she said to Balaam:

"Why have you struck me? Have I not always obeyed you?"

Balaam was so astonished, he did not know what to think. But just then, God opened his eyes so that he, too, saw the angel standing in the road. Balaam fell to his knees, for he knew this was the angel of the Lord!

"Now, go with the men," cried the angel, "but remember to say only what God tells you to say!"

King Balak came to meet Balaam, and told him that he would give him much gold if he would curse the Israelites. But Balaam answered:

"I cannot curse these people unless God tells me to!"

Then King Balak took Balaam to a high mountain. Balaam looked down into the great valley below and saw the tents of the Children of Israel, row after row; and Balaam saw the Tabernacle Moses had set up.

Balaam stood looking down into the valley for a long time. King Balak waited and waited for the great prophet to put a curse upon these people who had camped outside his country.

But when Balaam finally opened his mouth to speak, Balak heard him say these words:

"How can I curse these people whom God has not cursed!"

King Balak was very angry. He took Balaam to another place and waited for him to speak. Once again Balaam opened his mouth, and spoke these words:

"God has commanded me to bless these people. For He has blessed them also. God brought the Children of Israel out of Egypt. These people shall rise up like a great lion and conquer the land!"

But Balak was not satisfied. He took Balaam to still another place, thinking surely this time the prophet would curse the Israelites. But for the third time, Balaam opened his mouth, and spoke these words:

"How goodly are thy tents, O Jacob, and thy tabernacles, O Israel! Blessed is he that blesseth thee, and cursed is he that curseth thee!"

When King Balak heard this, he was so angry that he shouted:

"Go on back to your home! I offered you all the gold and silver I possess to curse these Israelites! You have done nothing but bless them! Get out of my sight!"

The words of Balaam were true. The children of Israel did rise up like a mighty lion.

King Balak found out what many people never learn: that you cannot buy the blessing of God with money. God gives his blessings freely, to all those who obey His laws!

THE DEATH OF MOSES

On and on, for forty years, the Children of Israel wandered through the wilderness, with Moses leading them and always cheering them on and telling them not to give up hope.

Of all those who had come out of Egypt as men, the only ones living were Moses and Joshua and Caleb. Moses was now a hundred and twenty years old. He had lived forty years as a prince of Egypt, forty years as a shepherd in Midian, and forty years as the leader of Israel in the wilderness. But although he was so very old, God had kept up his strength. His eyes were bright, his mind was clear, and his arm and heart were strong.

The people of Israel now had full possession of all the land on the east of the river Jordan, from the brook Arnon up to the great Mount Hermon. Much of this land was well fitted for pasture; for grass was green and rich, and there were many streams of water. There were two of the twelve tribes and half of another tribe, whose people had great flocks of sheep and goats and herds of cattle. These were the tribes which had sprung from Reuben and Gad, the sons of Jacob, and half of the tribe of Manasseh, the son of Joseph. There were two tribes that had sprung from Joseph, his descendants, the tribes of Ephraim and Manasseh.

The men of Reuben, Gad, and half the men of Manasseh came to Moses and said:

"The land on this side of the river is good for the feeding of sheep and cattle; and we are shepherds and herdsmen. Cannot we have our possessions on this side of the river, and give all the land beyond the river to our brothers of the other tribes?"

Moses was not pleased at this, for he thought that the men of these tribes wished to have their home at once in order to avoid going to war with the rest of the tribes; and this may have been in their minds.

So Moses said to them:

"Shall your brothers of the other tribes go to the war, and shall you sit here in your own land and not help them? That would be wicked, and would displease the Lord your God." Then the men of the two tribes and the half-tribe came again to Moses, and said to him:

"We will build sheepfolds here for our sheep, and we will choose some cities in which to place our wives and our children; and we ourselves will go armed with our brothers of the other tribes, and will help them to take

the land on the other side of the Jordan. We will not come back to this side of the river until the war is over, and our brothers have taken their shares of the land, each tribe its own part; and we will take no part on the other side of the river because our place has been given to us here. And when the land is all won and divided, then we will come back here to our wives and our children."

Then Moses was satisfied with the promise that they had given, and he divided the land on the east of the Jordan among these tribes. To the men of Reuben he gave the land on the south; to the men of Gad the land in the middle; and to the half-tribe of Manasseh the land on the north, the country called Bashan. And after their wives and children and flocks had been placed safely, the men of war came to the camp, ready to go with the other tribes across the river when God should call them.

And now the work of Moses was almost done. God said to him:

"Gather the children of Israel together and speak your last words to them, for you are not to lead the people across the Jordan. You are to die in this land, as I said to you at Kadesh."

Then Moses called the leaders of the twelve tribes before his tent and said to them:

"I am now an old man. God has told me that I am not to lead you across the river Jordan. Joshua will lead you. He is a good man, and God has chosen him to be your new leader. You must do as Joshua commands, trust him always, and never forget to pray to God for help. Remember to thank Him, too, each morning and night, for the many blessings He has sent you. Remember how God fed you manna in the desert and brought forth water from rocks when you were thirsty, and gave us His own holy Laws to live by."

Then Moses stretched forth his hands and blessed the people he had led for so long and loved so dearly. The great leader of the Israelites looked at the crowd standing quietly before him. Some of these great strong men had been just small babies when Moses led them and their mothers and fathers out of Egypt so many years ago. Many of the parents had died, others were old and gray. Suddenly, Moses could not see the faces of his people clearly, because of the tears that filled his eyes.

Then he called Joshua to his side and said:

"Be strong and of good courage, for you must go with the people into the land which God has promised them. But fear not, the Lord will go before you and make the way easy. He will be with you all the time. Whenever you need help, bow down before the Lord your God and He will speak words of wisdom into your ears."

Then Moses, all alone, went out of the camp, while all the people wept. Slowly he walked up the mountainside, until they saw him no more. He climbed to the top of Mount Nebo, and stood alone upon the height, and

looked at the Land of Promise, which lay spread out before him. Far in the north he could see the white crown of Mount Hermon, where most of the year there is snow. At his feet, but far below, the river Jordan was winding its way down to the Dead Sea. Across the river, at the foot of the mountains, was standing the city of Jericho, surrounded by a high wall. On the summits of the mountains beyond he could see Hebron, where Abraham and Isaac, and Jacob were buried; he could see Jerusalem, and Bethel, and the two mountains where Shechem lay hidden in the center of the land. And here and there, through the valleys, he could see afar in the west the gleaming water of the Great Sea.

"Behold, Moses," God said, "before you lies the Promised Land! This is the land of milk and honey which I promised Abraham and Isaac and Jacob and all their children to come after them. But you will not cross the Jordan into this land, Moses. Your task is done. Now it is time for you to rest, for Joshua is young and strong and he will complete the task which you have done so well."

Moses bowed his head once more, but his heart was so full that he could not speak. Now he could die in peace. He knew that his beloved people would live in the Promised Land which God showed him, and that the hardest part of the great journey was over.

Moses, the great prophet and leader of his people, could rest at last. He lay down on the mountain's top, and died. There was no man on Mount Nebo to bury Moses; so God himself buried him, and no man knows where God laid the body of Moses, who had served God so faithfully.

And after Moses there was never a man who lived so near to God, and talked with God so freely, as one would talk face to face with another.

The Children of Israel wept and mourned for thirty days after the death of Moses. They knew in their hearts they would never have another leader as great as he had been, or as patient and kind.

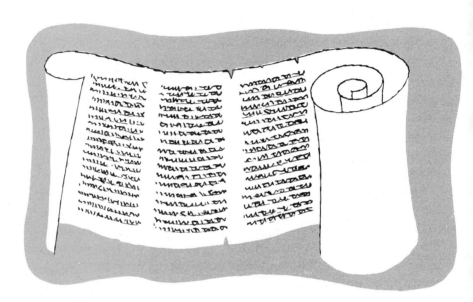